Science Essentials

ELEMENTARY LEVEL

Lessons and Activities for Test Preparation

Science Essentials

ELEMENTARY LEVEL

Lessons and Activities for Test Preparation

Mark J. Handwerker, Ph.D.

JOSSEY-BASS
A Wiley Imprint
www.josseybass.com

Library of Congress Cataloging-in-Publication Data

Handwerker, Mark J.
    [Ready-to-use science proficiency lessons & activities, 4th-grade level]
    Science essentials, elementary school level / Mark J. Handwerker.— 1st ed.
        p. cm. — (Science essentials series)
    Originally published: Ready-to-use science proficiency lessons & activities, 4th-grade
    level. Paramus, N.J. : Center for Applied Research in Education, c2001, in series:
    TestPrep curriculum activities library.
    ISBN 0-7879-7576-1 (alk. paper)
        1. Science—Study and teaching (Elementary)—United States.   2. Science—Study and
    teaching (Elementary)—Activity programs—United States.   3. Fourth grade
    (Education)—United States.   I. Title.

    LB1585.3.H36   2004
    372.3'5044—dc22
                                                                        2004045127

Printed in the United States of America
FIRST EDITION
PB Printing 10 9 8 7 6 5 4 3 2 1

About This Science TestPrep Teaching Resource

Science Essentials gives classroom science teachers and science specialists a dynamic and progressive way to meet curriculum standards and competencies. The lessons actively engage students in learning about the natural and technological world in which we live by encouraging them to use their senses and intuitive abilities on the road to discovery. The lessons and activities have been developed and tested by professional science teachers who sought to provide students with enjoyable learning experiences while at the same time preparing them for district and statewide science proficiency exams.

For quick access and easy use, materials are printed in a big 8¼" × 10⅞" lay-flat format that folds flat for photocopying of over 150 student activity sheets and are organized into the following four sections:

I. METHODS AND MEASUREMENT

Lessons 1 through 12 plus Sample Test Questions

II. PHYSICAL SCIENCE

Lessons 13 through 30 plus Sample Test Questions

III. LIFE SCIENCE

Lessons 31 through 45 plus Sample Test Questions

IV. EARTH SCIENCE

Lessons 46 through 62 plus Sample Test Questions

Each section includes 12 to 17 detailed lessons with reproducible student handouts for teaching basic concepts and skills in one important area of science. All of the lessons and student handouts are complete and ready for use. Each lesson includes:

- the **Basic Principle** underlying the lesson and accompanying student activity

- the specific science **Competency** students will demonstrate

- **Materials** needed to complete the activity

- easy-to-follow, illustrated **Procedure** for presenting the lesson and accompanying student activity handout

- **Observation & Analysis** describing the desired results and answers to the student activity

- a two-page, illustrated **Student Handout** with step-by-step directions for carrying out the activity and recording observations and conclusions

The lessons in each section are followed by a variety of sample test questions focusing on the concepts and skills emphasized in that section. These are designed to help students prepare for the types of questions they will be asked in actual test situations and are followed by complete answer keys.

Science Essentials are also available from the publisher for Middle School and High School levels. The lessons, activities, and sample test items in all three volumes provide a stimulating and effective way to help students master basic science content and prepare to demonstrate their knowledge.

Mark J. Handwerker, Ph.D.

About the Author

Mark J. Handwerker (B.S., C.C.N.Y.; Ph.D. in Biology, U.C.I.) has taught secondary school science for 18 years in the Los Angeles and Temecula Valley Unified School Districts. As a mentor and instructional support teacher, he has trained scores of new teachers in the "art" of teaching science. He is also the author/editor of articles in a number of scientific fields and the coauthor of an earth science textbook currently in use.

Dr. Handwerker teaches his students that the best way to learn basic scientific principles is to become familiar with the men and women who first conceived them. His classroom demonstrations are modeled on those used by the most innovative scientists of the past. He believes that a familiarity with the history of science, an understanding of the ideas and methods used by the world's most curious people, is the key to comprehending revolutions in modern technology and human thought.

Contents

About This Science TestPrep Teaching Resource v

Science Essentials

ELEMENTARY LEVEL

I. METHODS AND MEASUREMENT / 1

Lesson 1 3

Basic Principle: Differentiate observation from inference (interpretation).
Science Competency: Students will show that conclusions based on inference (interpretation) can be confirmed or contradicted by measurement.

Reproducibles: Student Handout—Lesson 1

Lesson 2 7

Basic Principle: Use the scientific method to test a prediction.
Science Competency: Students will show how the scientific method is used to test predictions.

Reproducibles: Student Handout—Lesson 2

Lesson 3 11

Basic Principle: Construct and interpret graphs and predictions.
Science Competency: Students will graph the heights of classmates to see which group is taller: boys or girls.

Reproducibles: Student Handout—Lesson 3

Lesson 4 15

Basic Principle: Measure and estimate length using English and Metric rulers.
Science Competency: Students will compare English and Metric measurement units for length.

Reproducibles: Student Handout—Lesson 4

Lesson 5 19

Basic Principle: Measure and estimate length using English and Metric rulers.
Science Competency: Students will measure the three dimensions of a rectangular box using English and Metric measurement units for length.

Reproducibles: Student Handout—Lesson 5

Lesson 6..**23**

Basic Principle: Measure and estimate surface area using English and Metric rulers.
Science Competency: Students will find the total surface area of a rectangular box using English and Metric measurement units for length and area.

Reproducibles: Student Handout—Lesson 6

Lesson 7..**27**

Basic Principle: Measure and estimate volume using English and Metric rulers.
Science Competency: Students will calculate the volume of a rectangular box using English and Metric measurement units for length.

Reproducibles: Student Handout—Lesson 7

Lesson 8..**31**

Basic Principle: Measure and estimate volume using Metric measures of volume.
Science Competency: Students will measure the volume of oddly shaped objects by water displacement.

Reproducibles: Student Handout—Lesson 8

Lesson 9..**35**

Basic Principle: Measure and estimate volume using Metric measures of volume.
Science Competency: Students will compare the calculated and measured volumes of wooden blocks.

Reproducibles: Student Handout—Lesson 9

Lesson 10..**39**

Basic Principle: Measure and estimate mass of objects using Metric measures of mass.
Science Competency: Students will measure the mass of objects using a balance.

Reproducibles: Student Handout—Lesson 10

Lesson 11..**43**

Basic Principle: Measure and estimate the mass of objects using Metric measures of mass.
Science Competency: Students will construct a balance to measure the mass of different objects.

Reproducibles: Student Handout—Lesson 11

Lesson 12..**47**

Basic Principle: Measure and estimate the density of objects using Metric measures of density.
Science Competency: Students will measure the density of different objects.

Reproducibles: Student Handout—Lesson 12

METHODS AND MEASUREMENT PRACTICE TEST

II. PHYSICAL SCIENCE / 59

Lesson 13..61

Basic Principle: Electricity and magnetism are related effects that have many useful applications in daily life.

Science Competency: Students will build a simple series circuit using wires, batteries, bulbs, and a switch. They will observe what happens when additional appliances (e.g., a second bulb) are added to a circuit powered by a single battery.

Reproducibles: Student Handout—Lesson 13

Lesson 14..65

Basic Principle: Electricity and magnetism are related effects that have many useful applications in daily life.

Science Competency: Students will build a simple series circuit using wires, batteries, bulbs, and a switch. They will observe what happens when the circuit is supplied with additional power (e.g., a second battery).

Reproducibles: Student Handout—Lesson 14

Lesson 15..69

Basic Principle: Electricity and magnetism are related effects that have many useful applications in daily life.

Science Competency: Students will build a simple parallel circuit using wires, batteries, bulbs, and a switch.

Reproducibles: Student Handout—Lesson 15

Lesson 16..73

Basic Principle: Electricity and magnetism are related effects that have many useful applications in daily life.

Science Competency: Students will show how the Earth's magnetic field can be detected by a bar magnet.

Reproducibles: Student Handout—Lesson 16

Lesson 17..77

Basic Principle: Electricity and magnetism are related effects that have many useful applications in daily life.

Science Competency: Students will show how to make a simple magnet.

Reproducibles: Student Handout—Lesson 17

Lesson 18..81

Basic Principle: Electricity and magnetism are related effects that have many useful applications in daily life.

Science Competency: Students will show how to make a simple compass.

Reproducibles: Student Handout—Lesson 18

Lesson 19...**85**

Basic Principle: Electricity and magnetism are related effects that have many useful applications in daily life.

Science Competency: Students will show that electric currents produce magnetic fields.

Reproducibles: Student Handout—Lesson 19

Lesson 20...**89**

Basic Principle: Electricity and magnetism are related effects that have many useful applications in daily life.

Science Competency: Students will build a simple electromagnet.

Reproducibles: Student Handout—Lesson 20

Lesson 21...**93**

Basic Principle: Electricity and magnetism are related effects that have many useful applications in daily life.

Science Competency: Students will build a simple motor to show how electrical energy can be changed to motion.

Reproducibles: Student Handout—Lesson 21

Lesson 22...**97**

Basic Principle: Electricity and magnetism are related effects that have many useful applications in daily life.

Science Competency: Students will examine the circuit used to make a doorbell ring.

Reproducibles: Student Handout—Lesson 22

Lesson 23...**101**

Basic Principle: Electricity and magnetism are related effects that have many useful applications in daily life.

Science Competency: Students will construct an electroscope to show that electrically charged objects repel each other.

Reproducibles: Student Handout—Lesson 23

Lesson 24...**105**

Basic Principle: Electricity and magnetism are related effects that have many useful applications in daily life.

Science Competency: Students will show that electrically charged objects repel each other.

Reproducibles: Student Handout—Lesson 24

Lesson 25...**109**

Basic Principle: Electricity and magnetism are related effects that have many useful applications in daily life.

Science Competency: Students will show that magnets have two poles.

Reproducibles: Student Handout—Lesson 25

Lesson 26..**113**

Basic Principle: Electricity and magnetism are related effects that have many useful applications in daily life.

Science Competency: Students will show that like poles of magnets repel one another while unlike poles attract.

Reproducibles: Student Handout—Lesson 26

Lesson 27..**117**

Basic Principle: Electricity and magnetism are related effects that have many useful applications in daily life.

Science Competency: Students will draw the magnetic field lines around a bar magnet to illustrate the force field surrounding it.

Reproducibles: Student Handout—Lesson 27

Lesson 28..**121**

Basic Principle: Electricity and magnetism are related effects that have many useful applications in daily life.

Science Competency: Students will demonstrate that electrical energy is quickly changed to heat energy.

Reproducibles: Student Handout—Lesson 28

Lesson 29..**125**

Basic Principle: Electricity and magnetism are related effects that have many useful applications in daily life.

Science Competency: Students will build a lightbulb to show how electrical energy is changed to light energy.

Reproducibles: Student Handout—Lesson 29

Lesson 30..**129**

Basic Principle: Electricity and magnetism are related effects that have many useful applications in daily life.

Science Competency: Students will build a battery to show how chemical energy is changed to electrical energy.

Reproducibles: Student Handout—Lesson 30

PHYSICAL SCIENCE PRACTICE TEST

III. LIFE SCIENCE / 141

Lesson 31..**143**

Basic Principle: All organisms need energy and matter to live and grow.

Science Competency: Students will show that plants are attracted to sunlight to obtain their energy.

Reproducibles: Student Handout—Lesson 31

Lesson 32...147

Basic Principle: All organisms need energy and matter to live and grow.
Science Competency: Students will show that plants deprived of sunlight cannot survive.

Reproducibles: Student Handout—Lesson 32

Lesson 33...151

Basic Principle: All organisms need energy and matter to live and grow.
Science Competency: Students will observe that plants make starch in the presence of sunlight.

Reproducibles: Student Handout—Lesson 33

Lesson 34...155

Basic Principle: All organisms need energy and matter to live and grow.
Science Competency: Students will identify foods that have starch, a primary food source for animals in the food chain.

Reproducibles: Student Handout—Lesson 34

Lesson 35...159

Basic Principle: Living organisms depend on one another for their survival.
Science Competency: Students will classify organisms as either producers or consumers of food.

Reproducibles: Student Handout—Lesson 35

Lesson 36...163

Basic Principle: Living organisms depend on one another for their survival.
Science Competency: Students will classify animals as herbivores, carnivores, or omnivores.

Reproducibles: Student Handout—Lesson 36

Lesson 37...167

Basic Principle: Living organisms depend on one another for their survival.
Science Competency: Students will construct a "food chain" to show that plants, herbivores, carnivores, and omnivores depend on one another for survival.

Reproducibles: Student Handout—Lesson 37

Lesson 38...171

Basic Principle: Living organisms depend on one another for their survival.
Science Competency: Students will draw a chart of a "food pyramid" to show how primary and secondary consumers compete for resources in an ecosystem.

Reproducibles: Student Handout—Lesson 38

Lesson 39...175

Basic Principle: Living organisms need energy and matter to live and grow.
Science Competency: Students will show that microorganisms cause decomposition.

Reproducibles: Student Handout—Lesson 39

Lesson 40...**179**

Basic Principle: Living organisms depend on one another for survival.
Science Competency: Students will discuss the eating habits of insects to explain how they help recycle dead matter from dead plants and animals to living organisms.

Reproducibles: Student Handout—Lesson 40

Lesson 41...**183**

Basic Principle: Living organisms depend on living and nonliving resources in the environment.
Science Competency: Students will list the living and nonliving resources in different ecosystems.

Reproducibles: Student Handout—Lesson 41

Lesson 42...**187**

Basic Principle: Living organisms depend on living and nonliving resources in the environment.
Science Competency: Students will discuss how the survival of living organisms depends on nonliving resources in the environment.

Reproducibles: Student Handout—Lesson 42

Lesson 43...**191**

Basic Principle: How well adapted organisms are to their environment determines how well they survive.
Science Competency: Students will show that for any particular environment some kinds of organisms survive well, some survive less well, and some cannot survive at all.

Reproducibles: Student Handout—Lesson 43

Lesson 44...**195**

Basic Principle: Living organisms depend on one another for survival.
Science Competency: Students will show that many microorganisms do not cause disease and can be beneficial to other living organisms.

Reproducibles: Student Handout—Lesson 44

Lesson 45...**199**

Basic Principle: Living organisms depend on one another for survival.
Science Competency: Students will show that many plants depend on insects and animals for pollination and seed dispersal.

Reproducibles: Student Handout—Lesson 45

LIFE SCIENCE PRACTICE TEST

IV. EARTH SCIENCE / 209

Lesson 46..211

Basic Principle: The properties of rocks and minerals reflect the processes that formed them. *Science Competency:* Students will define terms used to describe the methods of rock formation. They will use these terms to complete a diagram describing the rock cycle.

Reproducibles: Student Handout—Lesson 46

Lesson 47..215

Basic Principle: The properties of rocks and minerals reflect the processes that formed them. *Science Competency:* Students will tell the difference among igneous, sedimentary, and metamorphic rocks by examining their properties and discussing their methods of formation (the rock cycle).

Reproducibles: Student Handout—Lesson 47

Lesson 48..219

Basic Principle: The properties of rocks and minerals reflect the processes that formed them. *Science Competency:* Students will show that sedimentary rocks contain carbonates, a substance found commonly in the shells of sea creatures.

Reproducibles: Student Handout—Lesson 48

Lesson 49..223

Basic Principle: Rock size and composition determine how quickly rocks are broken down. *Science Competency:* Students will show that the size of rock particles can affect how quickly they are broken down by chemical action.

Reproducibles: Student Handout—Lesson 49

Lesson 50..227

Basic Principle: The properties of rocks and minerals reflect the processes that formed them. *Science Competency:* Students will construct paper models of different kinds of rock crystals.

Reproducibles: Student Handout—Lesson 50

Lesson 51..231

Basic Principle: The properties of rocks and minerals reflect the processes that formed them. *Science Competency:* Students will grow sodium bicarbonate crystals.

Reproducibles: Student Handout—Lesson 51

Lesson 52..235

Basic Principle: Identify common rock-forming minerals using a table of diagnostic properties. *Science Competency:* Students will identify the hardness of minerals using the Mohs Scale of Hardness.

Reproducibles: Student Handout—Lesson 52

Lesson 53..239

Basic Principle: The properties of rocks and minerals reflect the processes that formed them.
Science Competency: Students will show how the formation of cave stalagmites and stalactites occurs.

Reproducibles: Student Handout—Lesson 53

Lesson 54..243

Basic Principle: Wind can reshape the Earth's land surface.
Science Competency: Students will demonstrate how wind changes sand formations in deserts and beaches.

Reproducibles: Student Handout—Lesson 54

Lesson 55..247

Basic Principle: Water can reshape the Earth's land surface.
Science Competency: Students will demonstrate how water changes sand and soil formations.

Reproducibles: Student Handout—Lesson 55

Lesson 56..251

Basic Principle: Natural processes, including freezing and thawing, cause rocks to break.
Science Competency: Students will show that water expands when freezing.

Reproducibles: Student Handout—Lesson 56

Lesson 57..255

Basic Principle: Natural processes, including freezing and thawing, cause rocks to break.
Science Competency: Students will show that freezing water can break hard materials such as metals and rocks.

Reproducibles: Student Handout—Lesson 57

Lesson 58..259

Basic Principle: Some changes in the Earth are due to slow processes, such as weathering, erosion, and slow movement of Earth's crustal plates.
Science Competency: Students will show how the Earth's crustal plates move about on the surface of our planet.

Reproducibles: Student Handout—Lesson 58

Lesson 59..263

Basic Principle: Some changes in the Earth are due to slow processes, such as weathering, erosion, and slow movement of Earth's crustal plates.
Science Competency: Students will show how the Earth's crustal plates press together to form mountain ranges and folds.

Reproducibles: Student Handout—Lesson 59

Lesson 60..**267**

Basic Principle: Some changes in the Earth are due to rapid processes, such as landslides, volcanic eruptions, and earthquakes.

Science Competency: Students will show how the pressure builds up in volcanoes, resulting in their periodic eruptions.

Reproducibles: Student Handout—Lesson 60

Lesson 61..**271**

Basic Principle: Some changes in the Earth are due to slow processes, such as weathering, erosion, and slow movement of Earth's crustal plates.

Science Competency: Students will show how landforms are eroded by abrasion.

Reproducibles: Student Handout—Lesson 61

Lesson 62..**275**

Basic Principle: Some changes in the Earth are due to slow processes, such as weathering, erosion, and slow movement of Earth's crustal plates.

Science Competency: Students will show how different kinds of soil affect the flow of water through Earth landforms.

Reproducibles: Student Handout—Lesson 62

EARTH SCIENCE PRACTICE TEST

Appendix **287**
Preparing Your Students for Standardized Proficiency Tests

What Parents Need to Know about Standardized Tests   287   The Uses of Standardized Tests   288   Test Terms   289   Common Types of Standardized Tests   292   Preparing Your Child for Standardized Tests   294   Cover Letter to Parents Announcing Standardized Tests   295   What Students Need to Know about Standardized Tests   296   Test-Taking Tips for Students   297   Test Words You Should Know   298   Creating a Positive Test-Taking Environment   299

Science Essentials

ELEMENTARY LEVEL

Lessons and Activities for Test Preparation

Section I: Methods and Measurement

LESSONS AND ACTIVITIES

Lesson 1 Students will show that conclusions based on inference (interpretation) can be confirmed or contradicted by measurement.

Lesson 2 Students will show how the scientific method is used to test predictions.

Lesson 3 Students will graph the heights of classmates to see which group is taller: boys or girls.

Lesson 4 Students will compare English and Metric measurement units for length.

Lesson 5 Students will measure the three dimensions of a rectangular box using English and Metric measurement units for length.

Lesson 6 Students will find the total surface area of a rectangular box using English and Metric measurement units for length and area.

Lesson 7 Students will calculate the volume of a rectangular box using English and Metric measurement units for length.

Lesson 8 Students will measure the volume of oddly shaped objects by water displacement.

Lesson 9 Students will compare the calculated and measured volumes of wooden blocks.

Lesson 10 Students will measure the mass of different objects using a balance.

Lesson 11 Students will construct a balance to measure the mass of different objects.

Lesson 12 Students will measure the density of different objects.

METHODS AND MEASUREMENT PRACTICE TEST

Lesson 1: Teacher Preparation

Basic Principle   Differentiate observation from inference (interpretation).

Competency   Students will show that conclusions based on inference (interpretation) can be confirmed or contradicted by measurement.

Materials   ruler

Procedure

1. Discuss with students some of the periodicities found in nature: the movements of the sun, moon, and planets; the changing phases of the moon; the regularity in the change of seasons. Mention that people have always been curious about these natural events and have used their five senses (e.g., sight, hearing, smell, touch, and taste) to try to understand the workings of nature. Point out, however, that our senses are not perfect and not always reliable.

2. Have students refer to Figure A on STUDENT HANDOUT—LESSON 1. By looking carefully at the figure they will discover that they can make either corner of the cube pop out at them. This is an optical illusion that makes the figure appear three-dimensional when it is actually a two-dimensional drawing.

3. Have students refer to Figure B on STUDENT HANDOUT—LESSON 1. By looking carefully at the figure they will discover they can see either six blocks "right side up" or seven blocks "upside down." If, at first, they have trouble seeing the seven upside-down blocks, instruct them to turn the figure upside down. They can then turn the figure right-side up and try to see the seven blocks again.

4. They should mention in their short paragraph that the senses (e.g., sight) sometimes have trouble processing information about the environment.

Observations & Analysis

- The bottom line in the first figure appears longer than the top line; but, careful measurement will show both lines are of equal length.

- The two horizontal lines in the second illusion appear bent; but, careful measurement will show they are parallel straight lines.

- The diagonal lines in the third figure appear crooked; but, careful measurement will show they are parallel straight lines.

Careful measurement will show that both lines are 2-1/32 inches, or 5.1 centimeters, long.

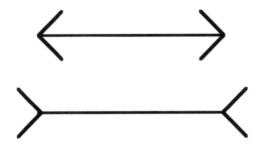

Careful measurement will show that both lines are 19/32 inches, or 1.5 centimeters, apart along their entire length as measured from inside the lines.

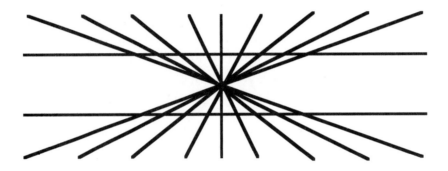

Careful measurement will show that both lines are 21/32 inches, or 1.7 centimeters, apart along their entire length as measured from inside the lines.

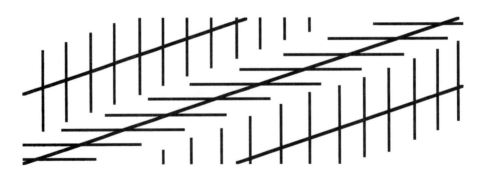

Name _____ **Date** _____

Methods and Measurement
STUDENT HANDOUT–LESSON 1

Basic Principle   Differentiate observation from inference (interpretation).

Objective   Show that conclusions based on inference (interpretation) can be confirmed or contradicted by measurement.

Materials   ruler

Procedure

1   Examine the pictures shown below.

2.   Write a short paragraph about how well your senses process information about the environment.

Figure A
Which corner pops out at you: A or B?

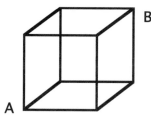

Figure B
Are the blocks right-side up or down?

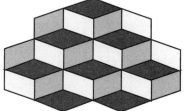

_____

_____

_____

_____

_____

3.   Complete the *Observations & Analysis* section.

Observations & Analysis

1.   Examine the lines shown here. Which line appears longer: top or bottom?

Use a ruler to measure the length of each line from one end to the other. Is one line longer than the other? Or, are the lengths of the lines the same?

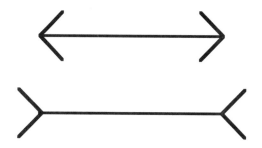

_____

2. Examine the horizontal lines shown below. Do they appear bent or straight?

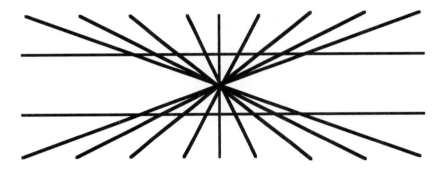

Use a ruler to measure the distance between the lines at several points. Does the distance between them change? Based on your measurements, are the lines bent or straight?

_____

3. Examine the figure shown below. Are the diagonal lines crooked or parallel?

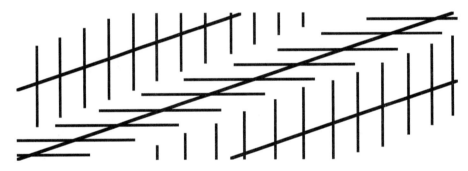

Use a ruler to measure the distance between the lines at several points. Does the distance between them change? Based on your measurements, are the lines crooked or parallel?

_____

4. Write a sentence about the reliability of your senses to process information about the environment.

_____

_____

_____

_____

_____

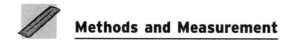

Lesson 2: Teacher Preparation

Basic Principle   Use the scientific method to test a prediction.

Competency   Students will show how the scientific method is used to test predictions.

Materials   baking soda, sugar, salt, white vinegar, water, rubbing alcohol (or other relatively harmless clear liquid), small glasses or beakers, large pitcher or beaker, small bowls or petri dishes, teaspoons, paper towels

Procedure

1. Begin the lesson by discussing the importance of making careful observations. Instruct students to watch your demonstration carefully, so that they can report exactly what you did after it is over. Perform the following simple demonstration: (1) Pour a few tablespoons of baking soda into a large pitcher or beaker. (2) Pour about one-half cup of white vinegar into the pitcher. Ask students to report what happened when you added the vinegar to the baking soda. They will report that bubbles were formed. Ask them if changing the order in which you mixed the chemicals might change the result. Do it. The bubbles will still be produced. Ask them if they think all white powders, such as sugar or salt, would behave this way when mixed with white vinegar. That question will serve as the problem stated in Step 1 of the Scientific Method outlined on STUDENT HANDOUT—LESSON 2.

2. Assist students in performing the procedure on STUDENT HANDOUT—LESSON 2. Then, assist them in designing an experiment to answer the question posed on the handout.

3. The following steps illustrate how the SCIENTIFIC METHOD might be used in answering the question posed.

   • **State the problem in the form of a question:** Do all clear liquids produce bubbles when mixed with baking soda?

   • **Gather information:** Students may include anything they know about any of the chemicals used in the experiment.

   • **State a hypothesis in the form of a simple statement:** (NOTE: Either of the following hypotheses is acceptable.) All clear liquids produce bubbles when mixed with baking soda. *Or* Not all clear liquids produce bubbles when mixed with baking soda.

- **Experiment:** Students' lists of materials may vary. The following is a list of suggested materials.

  (a) *List materials:* baking soda, water, white vinegar, rubbing alcohol (or other clear liquids), teaspoon, small bowls or petri dishes.

  (b) *Explain step-by-step procedure:* (i) Place one teaspoon of baking soda into each of three small bowls. (ii) Pour a teaspoon of vinegar into one bowl. (iii) Pour a teaspoon of water into the second bowl. (iv) Pour a teaspoon of rubbing alcohol into the third bowl.

  (c) *Describe what you observed during your experiment:* Only the white vinegar produced lots of bubbles when mixed with the baking soda. (NOTE: A small amount of bubbles may appear on the surface of the other powders; but only the baking soda and vinegar mixture produces an obvious "chemical reaction.")

- **Form a conclusion by accepting or rejecting the hypothesis:** Not all clear liquids produce bubbles when mixed with baking soda.

Name _____ **Date** _____

Methods and Measurement
STUDENT HANDOUT–LESSON 2

Basic Principle   Use the scientific method to test a prediction.

Objective   Show how the scientific method is used to test predictions.

Materials   baking soda, sugar, salt, white vinegar, small glass or beaker, 3 small bowls or petri dishes, teaspoon, paper towel

Procedure   Follow the steps of the SCIENTIFIC METHOD listed below to test the prediction that baking soda, sugar, and salt all react the same when mixed with white vinegar.

1. *State the problem in the form of a question:* Do baking soda, sugar, and salt all react the same when mixed with vinegar?

2. *Gather information:* Describe the color and texture of the baking soda, sugar, and salt particles.

    _____

    _____

3. *Form a hypothesis in a simple statement:* Baking soda, sugar, and salt all react the same when mixed with vinegar.

4. *Experiment:*

    (a) *List materials*—baking soda, sugar, salt, white vinegar, small glass or beaker, 3 small bowls or petri dishes, teaspoon, paper towel

    (b) *Explain step-by-step procedure:* (i) Place one teaspoon of baking soda into a small bowl and clean the teaspoon with a paper towel. Place one teaspoon of sugar into a second small bowl and clean the teaspoon again. Place one teaspoon of salt into the third bowl and clean the teaspoon again. (ii) Pour vinegar into a small glass or beaker. (iii) Pour one level teaspoon of vinegar into each of the small bowls of white powder.

    (c) *Describe what you observed during your experiment:* _____

    _____

    _____

5. *Form a conclusion:* Baking soda, sugar, and salt do not react the same when mixed with vinegar. The baking soda mixture produces a lot of bubbles while the sugar and salt mixtures do not.

Use the SCIENTIFIC METHOD to answer the following question: Does baking soda produce bubbles when mixed with all clear liquids?

1. State the problem in the form of a question.

   _____

2. Gather information.

   _____

3. State a hypothesis in the form of a simple statement.

   _____

4. Experiment.

   (a) *List materials:*

   _____

   _____

   (b) *Explain step-by-step procedure:*

   _____

   _____

   _____

   _____

   _____

   _____

   _____

   _____

   (c) *Describe what you observed during your experiment:*

   _____

   _____

   _____

   _____

5. Form a conclusion by accepting or rejecting the hypothesis.

   _____

   _____

   _____

   _____

Lesson 3: Teacher Preparation

Basic Principle   Construct and interpret graphs and predictions.

Competency   Students will graph the heights of classmates to see which group is taller: boys or girls.

Materials   rulers, girls and boys

Procedure

1. Begin by discussing the fact that all human beings share many common characteristics. Yet, no two are exactly alike. Even identical twins, although they look very similar, may have totally different personalities. Tell students to look around the classroom and briefly identify some of the commonalities and differences among their classmates. Conclude that human beings come in many shapes and sizes, skin colors, and physical abilities. Since it is not possible to study every individual in a population (e.g., the entire human race), scientists study "sample populations" they believe to be representative of the whole group. They use tables, charts, and graphs to display the results of their investigation. Tables, charts, and graphs make it easier to "visualize" the commonalities and differences among the individuals of a population. Scientists study all kinds of populations: populations of plants, populations of animals, populations of stars.

2. Draw Graph A and Graph B to illustrate how some graphs summarize the characteristics of populations. For example, these graphs might represent the performance of students on a test. Graph A is a "normal population" because most of the individuals measured (e.g., tested) are in the middle of the population. Graph B is a "skewed population" because most of the individuals measured (e.g., tested) accumulated on one side of the graph.

3. Assist students in performing the procedure on STUDENT HANDOUT— LESSON 3.

Observations & Analysis

- Student graphs will vary according to their heights. However, both boys and girls should be distributed in somewhat normal populations. The overlapping arrangement of the bars helps to visualize the fact that both groups of individuals lie in the same approximate range and that the populations as a whole do not differ considerably. One could conclude, therefore, that the height of fourth-grade boys is generally the same as the height of fourth-grade girls.

- Refer to the SAMPLE DISTRIBUTIONS.

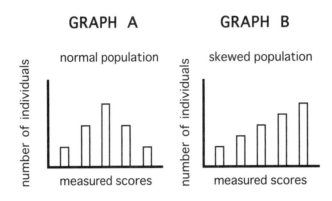

GRAPH A

normal population

number of individuals

measured scores

GRAPH B

skewed population

number of individuals

measured scores

SAMPLE DISTRIBUTIONS

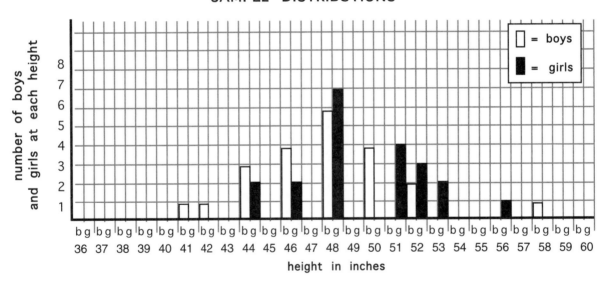

Methods and Measurement

STUDENT HANDOUT–LESSON 3

Basic Principle   Construct and interpret graphs and predictions.

Objective   Graph the heights of classmates to see which group is taller: girls or boys.

Materials   ruler, girls and boys

Procedure

1. Copy the names of the girls and boys listed on the board in the *Observations & Analysis* section.

2. Use a ruler to measure the height of the boys and girls in your group. If you are using an English ruler, change all measurements to inches. For example, 4 feet and 3 inches = 51 inches (4 feet × 12 inches per foot = 48 inches; 48 inches + 3 inches = 51 inches). If you are using a Metric ruler, simply record the person's height in centimeters.

3. Record your results on the board so that everyone can copy the same information. Then, copy all of the information.

4. Find the height of the shortest and tallest boy and girl. This information will help you to graph the correct range of heights on the horizontal axis of the graph in the *Observations & Analysis* section. Number the horizontal axis in inches (or centimeters) beginning with the shortest boy or girl.

5. Make separate bar graphs at each height for both boys and girls using the legend in the upper right-hand corner of the graph.

6. Complete the *Observations & Analysis* section.

Observations & Analysis

Girl's Name	Height	Girl's Name	Height	Boy's Name	Height	Boy's Name	Height
___	___	___	___	___	___	___	___
___	___	___	___	___	___	___	___
___	___	___	___	___	___	___	___
___	___	___	___	___	___	___	___
___	___	___	___	___	___	___	___
___	___	___	___	___	___	___	___
___	___	___	___	___	___	___	___
___	___	___	___	___	___	___	___
___	___	___	___	___	___	___	___
___	___	___	___	___	___	___	___

number of boys and girls at each height

□ = boys

■ = girls

b g | b g | b g | b g | b g | b g | b g | b g | b g | b g | b g | b g | b g | b g | b g | b g | b g | b g | b g | b g | b g

height in inches (or centimeters)

Write a short paragraph to summarize your results. Interpret your results to include the following information: Does the graph clearly show which group was taller? If so, then which group was taller: boys or girls? If not, then why not? What additional information would you need to find out which group is taller?

_____

_____

_____

_____

_____

_____

_____

Lesson 4: Teacher Preparation

Basic Principle   Measure and estimate length using English and Metric rulers.

Competency   Students will compare English and Metric measurement units for length.

Materials   English and Metric rulers, classroom items

Procedure

1. Begin with a discussion of the problems early humans must have had trying to measure and describe the size of objects, such as rocks, trees, and animals. The problems they encountered, until several thousand years ago, were largely due to the fact that primitive societies did not have a "standard" unit of length by which to compare one another's measurements. The Ancient Mesopotamians, Egyptians, and Greeks used standards such as the "cubit." A cubit is the length of a person's forearm from the elbow to fingertips. Ask students to discuss the difficulties ancient people might have had trying to build a house using this type of standard. Point out that all modern measurements rely upon a single "standard," such as the yard or meter, upon which everyone can agree. A universal standard allows an observer to compare his or her results to that of other observers. Scientific "objectivity" depends on the use of "standard units of measure."

2. Introduce some of the basic standard units for measuring length used in the English System of Measurement (e.g., inch, foot, yard, mile). Introduce some of the basic standard units for measuring length used in the Metric System of Measurement (e.g., millimeter, centimeter, meter, kilometer).

3. Assist students in performing the activity on STUDENT HANDOUT—LESSON 4 by leading an examination of English and Metric rulers.

Observations & Analysis

- Students will observe that careful measurement produces a "conversion factor" of about ($\approx$) 2.5 centimeters per inch for each object measured.

- *Answers to problems:* Student answers may vary slightly since the more accurate conversion factor is $\approx$ 2.54 cm per inch.

    (A) $\approx$ 12.5 cm   (B) $\approx$ 4 inches   (C) $\approx$ 17.5 cm   (D) $\approx$ 14 inches   (E) $\approx$ 30 cm

    (F) $\approx$ 16 inches   (G) $\approx$ 63 cm   (H) $\approx$ 20 inches   (I) $\approx$ 110 cm   (J) $\approx$ 40 inches

Changing Inches to Centimeters

How many centimeters are there in 10 inches? Since there are 2.5 centimeters in one inch . . .

$$
\begin{array}{r}
10 \ \text{inches} \\
\times \ 2.5 \ \text{cm per inch} \\
\hline
25 \ \text{cm}
\end{array}
$$

Changing Centimeters to Inches

How many inches are there in 25 centimeters? Since there are 2.5 centimeters in one inch . . .

$$
\begin{array}{r}
25 \ \text{inches} \\
\div \ 2.5 \ \text{cm per inch} \\
\hline
10 \ \text{inches}
\end{array}
$$

Name _____ Date _____

Methods and Measurement
STUDENT HANDOUT–LESSON 4

Basic Principle   Measure and estimate length using English and Metric rulers.

Objective   Compare English and Metric measurement units for length.

Materials   English and Metric rulers, classroom items

Procedure

1. Examine the English/Metric ruler shown below.

2. Note that the English side of the ruler uses inches. Since the English System of Measurement uses fractions, the inches are divided into halves (1/2), quarters (1/4), and eighths (1/8) of an inch.

3. Note that the Metric side of the ruler uses centimeters (cm). Since the Metric System of Measurement uses decimals, each centimeter is divided into ten equal parts called millimeters (mm). One millimeter is equal to 0.1 cm (1/10 cm).

4. Use an English/Metric ruler to measure the lengths of ten different items in the classroom, such as the length of your notebook, the classroom, your desk, and so on.

5. Record your data in the *Observations & Analysis* section.

6. Complete the *Observations & Analysis* section.

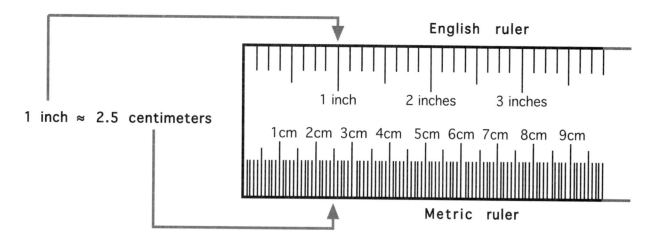

Observations & Analysis   Measure and record the lengths of different items. Change all English measure of feet and inches to inches only. For example, 2 feet and 7 inches = 31 inches (2 feet × 12 inches per foot = 24 inches; and, 24 inches + 7 inches = 31 inches). Find the number of centimeters per inch in the last column by dividing the number of centimeters by the number of inches.

item	centimeters (cm)	inches (in)	cm/in

Fill in the blanks below using the fact that there are about (≈) 2.5 centimeters per inch.

(A) 5 inches ≈ _____ cm

(B) _____ inches ≈ 10 cm

(C) 7 inches ≈ _____ cm

(D) _____ inches ≈ 36 cm

(E) 12 inches ≈ _____ cm

(F) _____ inches ≈ 40 cm

(G) 25 inches ≈ _____ cm

(H) _____ inches ≈ 50 cm

(I) 44 inches ≈ _____ cm

(J) _____ inches ≈ 100 cm

Lesson 5: Teacher Preparation

Basic Principle   Measure and estimate length using English and Metric rulers.

Competency   Students will measure the three dimensions of a rectangular box using English and Metric measurement units for length.

Materials   English and Metric rulers, rectangular blocks of wood or empty cardboard boxes

Procedure

1. Draw the illustration to illustrate the difference among length, area, and volume. Explain that "length" is a measure of one dimension of space. "Area" is a measure of two dimensions of space. "Volume" is a measure of three dimensions of space. Length can be measured in inches or centimeters. Area can be measured in "square inches" or "square centimeters." Volume can be measured in "cubic inches" or "cubic centimeters."

2. Assist students in performing the activity on STUDENT HANDOUT—LESSON 5.

Observations & Analysis

- Results will vary depending upon the dimensions of the wooden blocks or cardboard boxes students measure. Circulate around the classroom to make sure students are using their rulers correctly.

- Students should estimate the dimensions of the meteorite in the "imaginary box" in the same way they measured the dimensions of the cube on the front of their handout.

THE THREE DIMENSIONS OF SPACE

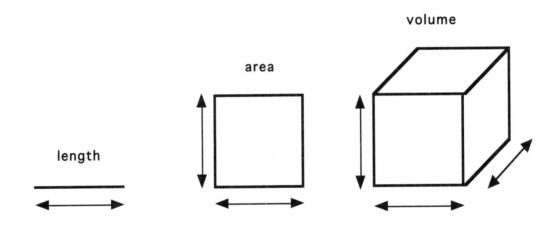

Name _____ **Date** _____

Methods and Measurement
STUDENT HANDOUT–LESSON 5

Basic Principle   Measure and estimate length using English and Metric rulers.

Objective   Measure the three dimensions of a rectangular box using English and Metric measurement units for length.

Materials   English and Metric rulers, blocks of wood or empty cardboard boxes

Procedure

1. Examine the diagram below. Use an English/Metric ruler to measure the three dimensions of the cube in inches and centimeters.

2. Complete the *Observations & Analysis* section.

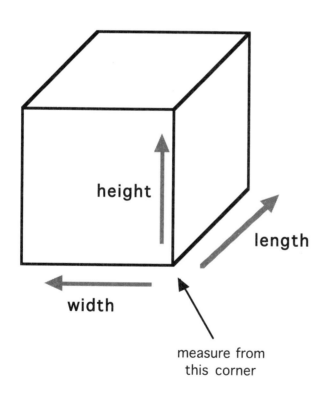

	inches	cm
length	_____	_____
width	_____	_____
height	_____	_____

Observations & Analysis   Using an English/Metric ruler, measure the length, width, and height of five rectangular boxes. Remember to begin all measurements from one corner of each box. To avoid confusion, make the longest side the length. Measure the other side lying flat on the table as the width. The last side that points to the ceiling is the box's height.

box number	length in : cm		width in : cm		height in : cm	

Imagine that the small meteorite shown below is in a perfectly rectangular box. Use your ruler to estimate the three dimensions of the rock.

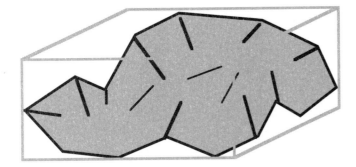

	inches	cm
length	_____	_____
width	_____	_____
height	_____	_____

Lesson 6: Teacher Preparation

Basic Principle Measure and estimate surface area using English and Metric rulers.

Competency Students will find the total surface area of a rectangular box using English and Metric measurement units for length and area.

Materials English and Metric rulers, rectangular blocks of wood or empty cardboard boxes

Procedure

1. Review the information covered in LESSON 5 in order to remind students that space has three dimensions. Draw the illustration. Show students how to calculate the area of the rectangle shown.

2. Ask students to consider how much wrapping paper it would take to completely and precisely cover the outside surface of a particular wooden block or box. That amount is equal to the "total surface area" of the object.

3. Assist students in performing the activity on STUDENT HANDOUT—LESSON 6.

Observations & Analysis

- Results will vary depending upon the dimensions of the wooden blocks or cardboard boxes students measure. Circulate around the classroom to make sure students are using their rulers correctly.

- *Answer to the question:* Students should explain that the meteorite has an odd shape that is not perfectly rectangular. Their measurements, therefore, are merely an approximation of the rock's actual surface area. The meteorite may have more or less surface area than the calculated surface area depending upon how smooth or rough its surface is.

CALCULATING THE AREA OF A RECTANGLE

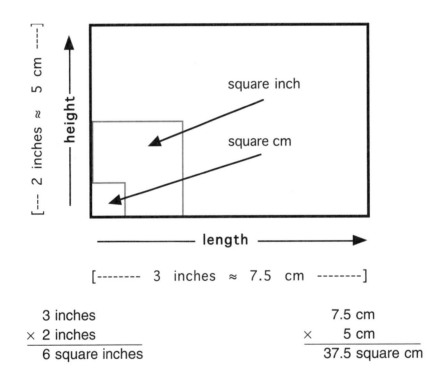

3 inches	7.5 cm
× 2 inches	× 5 cm
6 square inches	37.5 square cm

Methods and Measurement
STUDENT HANDOUT–LESSON 6

Basic Principle   Measure and estimate surface area using English and Metric rulers.

Objective   Find the total surface area of a rectangular box using English and Metric measurement units for length and area.

Materials   English and Metric rulers, blocks of wood or empty cardboard boxes

Procedure

1. Examine the diagram below. How many faces does the cube have? _____

2. Label the front side of the cube "Front Face."

3. Label the other sides as follows: Back Face, Right-Side Face, Left-Side Face, Top Face, and Bottom Face.

4. Find the "area" of the Front Face by measuring the length of two sides that are joined at a corner of that face. Then, multiply the two lengths to give the area of the Front Face. Measurements of lengths in inches give "square inches" as a unit of measure for area. Measurements of lengths in centimeters give "square centimeters" as a unit of measure for area.

5. Complete the *Observations & Analysis* section.

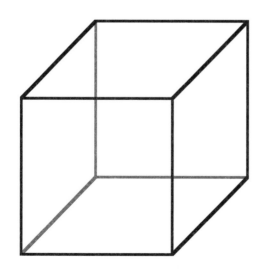

Area of Front Face

	in	cm
one side length	_____	_____
other side length	_____	_____
area in square inches	_____	
area in square centimeters		_____

Observations & Analysis

1. Use an English/Metric ruler to measure the length (l), width (w), and height (h) of four rectangular boxes. Find the area of each face. Add the area of all the faces to find the total surface area of each box.

Box Number	Face #1 (l x w) in : cm		Face #2 (l x h) in : cm		Face #3 (w x h) in : cm		Face #4 (l x w) in : cm		Face #5 (l x h) in : cm		Face #6 (w x h) in : cm		Total Surface Area	

2. Imagine that the small meteorite shown below is in a perfectly rectangular box. Use your ruler to estimate the total surface area of the rock.

<u>Show your math work here</u>.

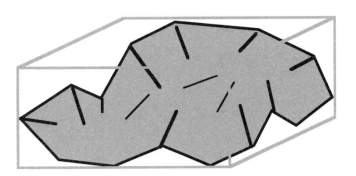

3. Explain why the actual surface area of the rock is probably different from your estimate.

_____

_____

_____

Lesson 7: Teacher Preparation

Basic Principle   Measure and estimate volume using English and Metric rulers.

Competency   Students will calculate the volume of a rectangular box using English and Metric measurement units for length.

Materials   English and Metric rulers, rectangular blocks of wood or empty cardboard boxes

Procedure

1. Review the information covered in LESSON 5 and LESSON 6 in order to remind students that space has three dimensions.

2. Assist students in performing the activity on STUDENT HANDOUT—LESSON 7. Use the illustration to explain why there are 64 small cubes in the large cube shown on their handout.

Observations & Analysis

- Results will vary depending upon the dimensions of the wooden blocks or cardboard boxes students measure. Circulate around the classroom to make sure students are using their rulers correctly.

- *Answer to the question:* Students should explain that the meteorite has an odd shape that is not perfectly rectangular. Their measurements, therefore, are merely an approximation of the rock's actual volume area.

CALCULATING THE VOLUME OF A CUBE

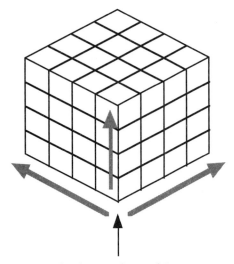

count the boxes from this corner

The large cube is 4 small cubes long, 4 small cubes wide, and 4 small cubes high.

Therefore . . .

$4 \times 4 = 16$,

and . . .

$4 \times 16 = \underline{64 \text{ cubes}}$.

Name _____ **Date** _____

Methods and Measurement
STUDENT HANDOUT–LESSON 7

Basic Principle Measure and estimate volume using English and Metric rulers.

Objective Calculate the volume of a rectangular box using English and Metric measurement units for length.

Materials English and Metric rulers, blocks of wood or empty cardboard boxes

Procedure

1. Examine the diagram below. How many small cubes are in the large cube? You can assume that the cube is perfectly rectangular. Then, count the small cubes that make up the length, width, and height of the cube. Remember to begin counting the small cubes from the same corner for each measurement. _____

2. The amount of space occupied by any three-dimensional object like this cube is called "volume." Volume is measured in "cubic inches" or "cubic feet" in the English System. Volume is measured in "cubic centimeters" or "cubic meters" in the Metric System.

3. Complete the *Observations & Analysis* section.

<u>Show your math work here.</u>

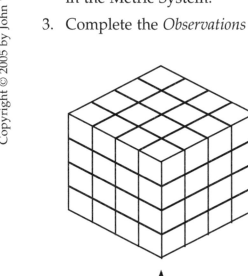

count the boxes from this corner

Observations & Analysis

1. Use an English/Metric ruler to measure the length (l), width (w), and height (h) of five rectangular boxes. Find the volume of each box by multiplying its length by its width by its height.

Box Number	length in : cm		width in : cm		height in : cm		volume (cu. inches)	volume (cu. cm)

2. Imagine that the small meteorite shown below is in a perfectly rectangular box. Use your ruler to estimate the volume of the rock.

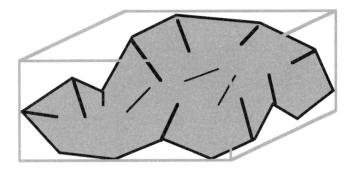

Show your math work here.

3. Explain why the actual volume of the rock is probably different from your estimate.

_____

_____

_____

_____

Lesson 8: Teacher Preparation

Basic Principle   Measure and estimate volume using Metric measures of volume.

Competency   Students will measure the volume of oddly shaped objects by water displacement.

Materials   2-liter plastic bottle of soda, small oddly shaped objects, graduated cylinders of varying sizes (e.g., 100 mL, 250 mL, 500 mL, 1,000 mL), water

Procedure

1. Show students the label on a 2-liter plastic bottle of soda. The amount of liquid in the bottle is shown on the label which reads "2 LITERS = 67.6 FLUID OUNCES = 2 QUARTS 3.6 FLUID OUNCES." Point out that in the Metric System of Measurement, the standard unit of measure for liquid volume is called the "liter" (L). Liquid volumes in the English System of Measurement are measured in "quarts" or "fluid ounces."

2. Explain that a liter can be divided into smaller units called "milliliters" (mL). There are 1,000 mL in one liter. To measure the volume of solids, scientists use the cubic centimeter. One cubic centimeter has the same volume as one milliliter.

3. Ask students what happens to the level of water in a bathtub when they sit in the tub. Explain that the amount that the water rises is equal to the volume of their body submerged in the tub. The great Greek mathematician, Archimedes (287 B.C.E.—212 B.C.E.)*, was the first to use this helpful fact to measure the volumes of oddly shaped objects that cannot be derived from measurement and calculation (e.g., length × width × height).

4. Demonstrate how to measure the volume of oddly shaped objects by water displacement. First, fill a graduated cylinder with water to a known amount. Record the amount of water in the cylinder. Then, totally submerge the oddly shaped object. Record the new amount. Subtract the reading of the known amount from the new reading. The difference equals the volume of the object.

5. Have students examine the illustration on the STUDENT HANDOUT and estimate the volume of the rock in the picture (*Answer*: 45 mL – 25 mL = 20 mL or 20 cubic cm).

6. Assist students in performing the activity on STUDENT HANDOUT—LESSON 8.

Observations & Analysis

- Results will vary depending upon the dimensions of the oddly shaped objects used in the activity. Circulate around the classroom to make sure students are reading the graduated cylinders correctly.

- *Answer to the question:* Students should explain that the graduated cylinders, like all other measuring tools, are only accurate within a given range. For example, a graduated cylinder with divisions set 5 mL apart is only accurate to the nearest 5 mL.

*B.C.E. = before common era.

MEASURING THE VOLUME OF AN ODDLY SHAPED OBJECT BY WATER DISPLACEMENT

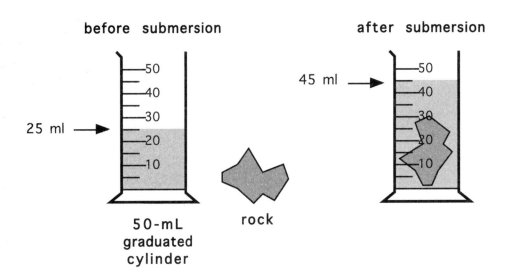

before submersion

after submersion

25 ml →

45 ml →

50-mL
graduated
cylinder

rock

Reading after submersion:	45 mL
Reading before submersion:	− 25 mL
Volume of rock:	20 mL or 20 cubic cm

Methods and Measurement
STUDENT HANDOUT–LESSON 8

Basic Principle   Measure and estimate volume using Metric measures of volume.

Objective   Measure the volume of oddly shaped objects by water displacement.

Materials   small oddly shaped objects, graduated cylinders of varying sizes, water

Procedure

1. Examine the picture shown below. Can you estimate the volume of the rock? Explain your reasoning. In the Metric System, volume is measured in "cubic centimeters" or "cubic meters." One cubic centimeter has the same volume as one "milliliter." There are 1,000 milliliters (mL) in one "liter (L)."

_____

_____

_____

_____

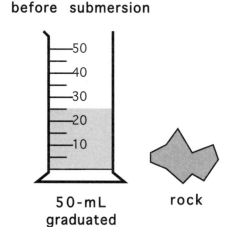

before submersion

50-mL
graduated
cylinder

rock

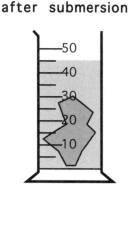

after submersion

2. Complete the *Observations & Analysis* section.

Observations & Analysis Use a graduated cylinder to find the volume of five oddly shaped objects by submerging the objects in a known amount of water.

object number	after submersion	before submersion	total volume

Show your math work here.

Explain why your measurements might not be exactly the same as the actual volume of the oddly shaped objects.

_____

_____

_____

_____

_____

_____

_____

_____

_____

_____

_____

_____

_____

Lesson 9: Teacher Preparation

Basic Principle   Measure and estimate volume using Metric measures of volume.

Competency   Students will compare the calculated and measured volumes of wooden blocks.

Materials   small wooden blocks (rectangular), Metric ruler, graduated cylinders of varying sizes (e.g., 100 mL, 250 mL, 500 mL, 1,000 mL), water

Procedure

1. Review LESSON 7 and LESSON 8 in order to remind students how to estimate and measure the volumes by calculation and water displacement.

2. Assist students in performing the activity on STUDENT HANDOUT—LESSON 9. Make sure all objects that float above the level of the water (e.g., blocks of wood) are forced down with a pencil or finger just under the surface of the water. These objects must be completely submerged before the final measurement is taken.

Observations & Analysis

- Results will vary depending upon the dimensions of the blocks used in the activity. Circulate around the classroom to make sure students are performing their measurements with accuracy.

- *Answer to the question:* Students should explain that all measuring tools are accurate to within a given range. Scientists realize that their measurements and calculations can only be as accurate as the measuring tools they use.

COMPARING THE VOLUME OF OBJECTS
USING TWO DIFFERENT METHODS OF MEASUREMENT

Volume determined by ruler measurement and calculation using the following formula:
Volume = length x width x height

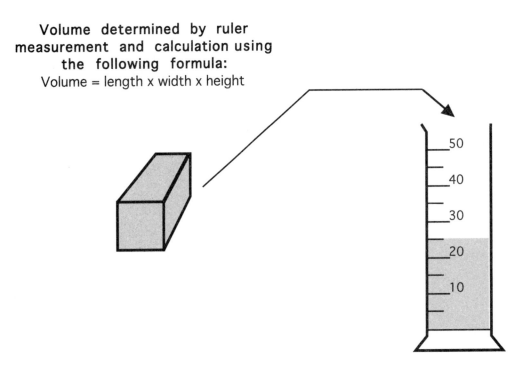

Volume determined by water displacement using the following formula:
Volume = volume of water after submersion
– volume of water before submersion

Name _____ **Date** _____

Methods and Measurement
STUDENT HANDOUT–LESSON 9

Basic Principle   Measure and estimate volume using Metric measures of volume.

Objective   Compare the calculated and measured volumes of wooden blocks.

Materials   small wooden blocks, graduated cylinders of varying sizes, Metric ruler, water

Procedure

1. Calculate the volumes of several small wooden blocks. Record your data in the table in the *Observations & Analysis* section.

2. Measure the volumes of the same blocks by water displacement. Record your data in the table in the *Observations & Analysis* section.

3. Complete the *Observations & Analysis* section.

Observations & Analysis Calculate the volumes of four small wooden blocks. Then, measure the volumes by water displacement. Subtract the lesser of the two volumes from the greater of the two volumes. The difference between the two estimates is called the "amount of error."

<u>Show your math work here.</u>

block number	calculated volume (cubic cm)	measured volume (mL)	amount of error

Explain why scientists always expect a small amount of "error" in their estimates, measurements, and calculations.

_____

_____

_____

_____

_____

_____

_____

_____

Lesson 10: Teacher Preparation

Basic Principle Measure and estimate the mass of objects using Metric measures of mass.

Competency Students will measure the mass of objects using a balance.

Materials small objects, balance

Procedure

1. Review the distinction between "mass" and "weight." Define mass as the amount of matter in an object. Define weight as the pull of gravity on an object. Remind students that astronauts in space are "weightless."

2. Explain that scientists measure the amount of matter in an object by comparing that object to a known standard mass called a "gram." A gram is the mass of one cubic centimeter (or a milliliter) of pure water at 4° Celsius at sea level.

3. Draw the top illustrations of different kinds of balances on the board and explain that the mass of objects is measured by "balancing them against the force of gravity." The mass (or amount of matter) in the unknown object is measured as equal to a known amount of standard objects, such as finely polished pebbles or a cubic centimeter of water (e.g., a gram).

4. Show students how to use and read the balance provided by your school. Assist students in performing the activity on STUDENT HANDOUT—LESSON 10.

Observations & Analysis

- Results will vary depending upon the objects used in the activity. Circulate around the classroom to make sure students are using and reading their balance correctly.

- *Answers to the questions*: Students should conclude that the size of an object is not necessarily a good indicator of its mass. A small object, such as a block or iron, may have more mass than a larger object, such as a big ball of cotton.

DIFFERENT TYPES OF BALANCES

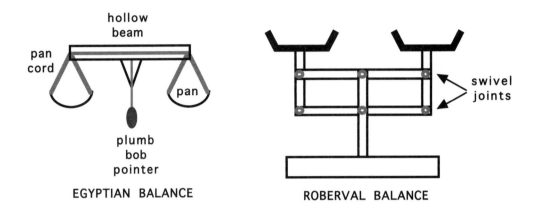

EGYPTIAN BALANCE

ROBERVAL BALANCE

The mass of objects is measured by balancing them against the force of gravity. The mass (or amount of matter) in the unknown object is equal to the known amount of standard objects such as a cubic centimeter of water (e.g., a gram).

TYPICAL DOUBLE-BEAM BALANCE

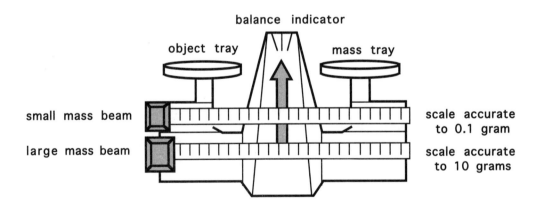

Name _____ **Date** _____

Methods and Measurement
STUDENT HANDOUT–LESSON 10

Basic Principle   Measure and estimate the mass of objects using Metric measures of mass.

Objective   Measure the mass of different objects using a balance.

Materials   small objects, balance

Procedure

1. Examine the picture of the typical double-beam balance shown below.

2. Compare the balance shown in the picture with the balance you will be using in this activity. Make sure you know how to read the scales on the balance before you begin. If you are not sure how to use the balance, ask your teacher for help.

3. Complete the *Observations & Analysis* section.

TYPICAL DOUBLE-BEAM BALANCE

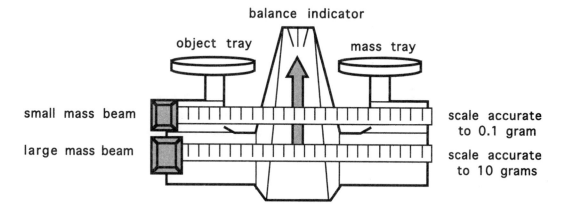

Observations & Analysis

1. Define mass: _____

   In the Metric System of Measurement, the unit of measurement for mass is called a "gram." This unit of measure is abbreviated with the letter "g." There are 1,000 grams in one "kilogram" (kg).

Object	mass (grams)

2. Use your balance to measure the mass of ten objects.

3. Which object contained the most matter? _____

4. Which object contained the least matter? _____

5. Do the larger objects always have more mass than the smaller objects?

   _____

6. Explain why the size of an object is not always a good indicator of its mass.

   _____

   _____

   _____

Lesson 11: Teacher Preparation

Basic Principle   Measure and estimate the mass of objects using Metric measures of mass.

Competency   Students will construct a balance to measure the mass of different objects.

Materials   small objects, pennies, classroom balance, cardboard, scissors, Metric ruler, pencil, tape, metal nut, string

Procedure   Assist students in performing the activity on STUDENT HANDOUT—LESSON 11.

Observations & Analysis   Results will vary depending upon the accuracy of each student's balance. However, students should be able to identify the flaws in their construction and suggest ways to improve the precision of their measuring tool.

COMMON PROBLEMS WITH STUDENT CARDBOARD BALANCES

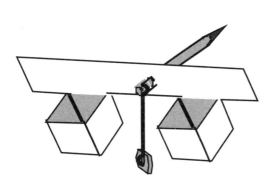

Pencil off center,
throwing tool off balance

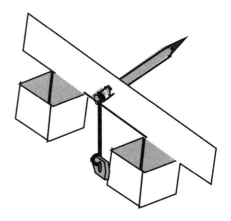

Pencil too snug in hole so
balance does not swing freely

Name _____ **Date** _____

Methods and Measurement
STUDENT HANDOUT–LESSON 11

Basic Principle   Measure and estimate the mass of objects using Metric measures of mass.

Objective   Construct a balance to measure the mass of different objects.

Materials   small objects, pennies, classroom balance, cardboard, scissors, Metric ruler, pencil, tape, metal nut, string

Procedure

1. Cut out a piece of cardboard measuring 20 × 30 centimeters as shown in the diagram. Draw squares measuring 5 × 5 centimeters on the cardboard. Mark dotted and solid lines as shown.

2. Cut *only* along dotted lines. Fold *only* along solid lines. Tape flaps to construct your balance as pictured.

3. Use a pencil to carefully punch out a hole at the exact top-center of the cardboard as shown. Insert the pencil and be sure the balance swings freely.

4. Tie a small metal nut to a piece of string. Suspend the string from the pencil. The string should hang straight down when your balance is horizontal to the floor. Draw a line on the cardboard along the length of the string.

5. Complete the *Observations & Analysis* section.

A CARDBOARD BALANCE

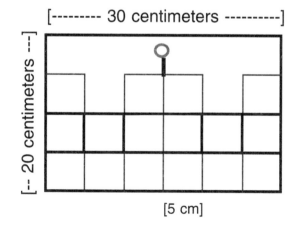

[--------- 30 centimeters ---------]

[-- 20 centimeters ---]

[5 cm]

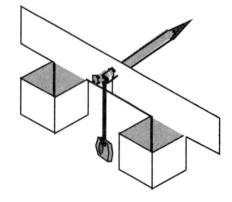

Observations & Analysis

1. Use a classroom balance to measure the mass of a single penny. _____

2. Use your cardboard balance to find the mass of ten small objects. Find the mass of each object by balancing it against as many pennies as you need. Multiply the number of pennies used by the mass of a single penny. The result is the mass of object.

object	mass of a single penny (g)	number of pennies used	object mass (g)

3. Explain how you could improve the accuracy of your cardboard balance.

_____

_____

_____

_____

_____

_____

_____

Lesson 12: Teacher Preparation

Basic Principle Measure and estimate the density of objects using Metric measures of density.

Competency Students will measure the density of different objects.

Materials small objects, classroom balance, graduated cylinders, water

Procedure

1. Ask students the following question: "Which object is heavier, a pound of iron or a pound of cotton?" Both objects have the same weight, of course, since they both weigh a pound. However, under normal circumstances the iron would take up less space, since the matter is more tightly packed inside a piece of iron than it is inside a piece of cotton. Under normal circumstances, a pound of cotton would occupy more space than a pound of iron. The measure of how tightly packed matter is inside an object is called "density." Define density as the "mass per unit volume of an object." Ask students to suggest ways of making the cotton as dense as the iron. They should suggest that the cotton could be compressed into a much smaller amount of space. If both the mass and volume of two substances are equal, then their densities are equal.

2. Show students how to calculate the density of an object by dividing its mass (e.g., measured on a balance) by its volume (measured by water displacement).

3. Assist students in performing the activity on STUDENT HANDOUT—LESSON 12. Make sure all objects that float above the level of the water (e.g., blocks of wood) are forced down with a pencil or finger just under the surface of the water. These objects must be completely submerged before the final measurement is taken.

Observations & Analysis

- Results will vary depending upon the objects used in the activity.
- *Answer to the question:* Saturn would float on water because it is a large ball of gas. The matter inside the giant planet is less densely packed than the matter inside a cup of water. The density of the planet Saturn is less than one gram per cubic centimeter.

THE PLANET SATURN WOULD FLOAT ON WATER

The mass of the planet Saturn
$\approx$ 700 billion billion billion grams

The volume of the planet Saturn
$\approx$ 1,000 billion billion billion cubic centimeters

700 billion billion billion grams
$\div$ 1,000 billion billion billion cubic centimeters

THE DENSITY OF SATURN
≈ 0.7
grams per cubic centimeter

Less than the density of water!!

Methods and Measurement
STUDENT HANDOUT–LESSON 12

Basic Principle   Measure and estimate the density of objects using Metric measures of density.

Objective   Measure the density of different objects.

Materials   small objects, classroom balance, graduated cylinders, water

Procedure

1. Copy the definition of the term "density."
2. Measure the mass of five small objects using a classroom balance.
3. Measure the volume of the same objects by water displacement.
4. Calculate the density of each object by dividing the mass of the object by its volume.

Observations & Analysis

1. Define density: _____

   _____

   _____

2. Find the mass and volume of five small objects. Then, calculate the density of each object.

object	mass (grams)	volume (ml = cu. cm)	density ($\frac{grams}{cu.\ cm}$)

3. The density of water is one gram per cubic centimeter. If the planet Saturn could be placed in a giant ocean filled with water, it would float. Explain how this is possible.

   _____

   _____

   _____

   _____

   _____

   _____

   _____

FOURTH-GRADE LEVEL

Methods and Measurement

PRACTICE TEST

Methods and Measurement

PRACTICE TEST

Directions: Use the Answer Sheet to darken the letter of the choice that best answers each question.

1. Which of the following is NOT a direct observation?

   (A) The spider is weaving a web.

   (B) The ruler is twelve inches long.

   (C) The sun is setting.

   (D) It must have rained because the sidewalk is wet.

   (E) There are five flowers in the vase.

2. Which is the best way to find out if the horizontal lines are bent or straight?

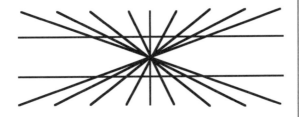

   (A) Measure the lengths of both lines.

   (B) Measure the distance between the lines at several points along their length.

   (C) Find out if the diagonal lines are straight.

   (D) Measure the distance between the lines at their center.

   (E) The lines must be bent because they look bent.

Matching: Show how you would use the steps of the scientific method to solve a problem. Use the Answer Sheet to darken the letter of the correct step to answer each question.

Steps of the Scientific Method

   (A) State a problem.

   (B) Gather information.

   (C) Form a hypothesis.

   (D) Experiment.

   (E) Form a conclusion.

3. Which step do you use when you go to the library to find out about ants and beetles?

4. Which step do you use when you ask the following question: "Which group of insects is more sensitive to light: ants or beetles?"

5. Which step do you use when you finally decide that ants are more sensitive to light than beetles?

6. Which step do you use when you guess that beetles are more sensitive to light than ants?

7. Which step do you use when you expose ants and beetles to light and measure how fast they seek dark shelter?

Directions: Two groups of students took a test. Use the bar graph of the two groups to answer questions 8 through 10. (Use the Answer Sheet.)

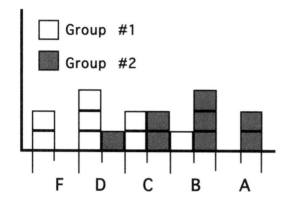

8. How many students are there in Group #1?

   (A) 6

   (B) 7

   (C) 8

   (D) 9

   (E) 10

9. How many students were tested?

   (A) 14

   (B) 15

   (C) 16

   (D) 17

   (E) 18

10. Based on the graph, which of the following is most likely true?

   (A) Group #1 did better on the test.

   (B) Group #2 did better on the test.

   (C) Both groups did about the same on the test.

   (D) Group #2 should have studied harder.

   (E) Group #1 didn't study.

Directions: Use the English/Metric ruler to answer questions 11 through 13. (Use the Answer Sheet.)

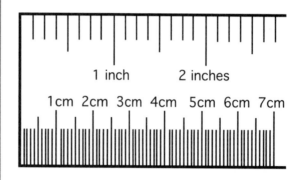

11. How many centimeters are there in 1 inch?

   (A) about 1.0

   (B) about 1.5

   (C) about 2.0

   (D) about 2.5

   (E) about 3.0

12. How many centimeters are there in 2 inches?

   (A) about 1

   (B) about 2

   (C) about 3

   (D) about 4

   (E) about 5

13. How many centimeters are there in 4 inches?

   (A) about 5

   (B) about 6

   (C) about 7

   (D) about 8

   (E) about 10

Directions: Use the solid cube shown below to answer questions 14 through 19. (Use the Answer Sheet.)

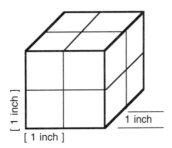

[1 inch]

1 inch

[1 inch]

14. What are the three dimensions of the cube?

    (A) 1 inch × 1 inch

    (B) 1 inch × 1 inch × 1 inch

    (C) 2 inches × 2 inches

    (D) 2 inches × 2 inches × 2 inches

    (E) 8 inches

15. What is the area of each face of the cube?

    (A) 2 inches

    (B) 4 inches

    (C) 2 square inches

    (D) 4 square inches

    (E) 8 square inches

16. What is the total surface area of the cube?

    (A) 12 inches

    (B) 12 square inches

    (C) 24 inches

    (D) 24 square inches

    (E) 24 cubic inches

17. How many small cubes are in the large cube?

    (A) 2

    (B) 4

    (C) 6

    (D) 8

    (E) 10

18. What is the volume of each small cube inside the large cube?

    (A) 1 inch

    (B) 4 inches

    (C) 6 inches

    (D) 1 square inch

    (E) 1 cubic inch

19. What is the volume of the large cube?

    (A) 4 square inches

    (B) 4 cubic inches

    (C) 8 square inches

    (D) 8 cubic inches

    (E) 24 square inches

Directions: Use the Answer Sheet to darken the letter of the choice that best answers each question.

20. Which of the following materials would work best to help you find the volume of an oddly shaped object?

    (A) an empty glass

    (B) a glass of water

    (C) a ruler

    (D) a bathroom scale

    (E) a calculator

21. The graduated cylinders shown below measure volume in milliliters or cubic centimeters. What is the volume of the rock?

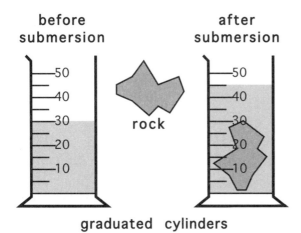

graduated cylinders

(A) 15 cubic centimeters

(B) 30 cubic centimeters

(C) 45 cubic centimeters

(D) 60 cubic centimeters

(E) 75 cubic centimeters

Directions: Use the diagram of the scale shown below to answer questions 22 through 25. (Use the Answer Sheet.)

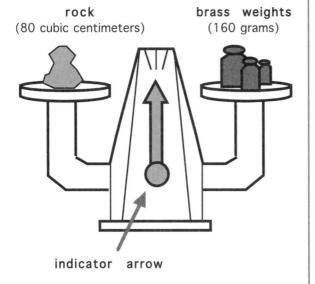

indicator arrow

22. What is the mass of the rock on the scale?

(A) 40 grams

(B) 80 grams

(C) 120 grams

(D) 160 grams

(E) Not enough information to answer the question.

23. If the rock were placed in a graduated cylinder, how much would the water rise?

(A) 40 milliliters

(B) 80 milliliters

(C) 120 milliliters

(D) 160 milliliters

(E) Not enough information to answer the question.

24. What is the density of the rock on the scale?

(A) 1 gram per cubic centimeter

(B) 2 grams per cubic centimeter

(C) 3 grams per cubic centimeter

(D) 4 grams per cubic centimeter

(E) 5 grams per cubic centimeter

25. Why is the "indicator arrow" pointing straight up?

(A) The rock is balanced by the brass weights.

(B) The volume of the rock is zero.

(C) The mass of the rock is zero.

(D) The density of the rock is zero.

(E) Not enough information to answer the question.

Methods and Measurement

PRACTICE TEST: ANSWER SHEET

Name _____   **Date** _____   **Period** _____

Darken the circle above the letter that best answers the question.

1. ○ A ○ B ○ C ○ D ○ E   14. ○ A ○ B ○ C ○ D ○ E

2. ○ A ○ B ○ C ○ D ○ E   15. ○ A ○ B ○ C ○ D ○ E

3. ○ A ○ B ○ C ○ D ○ E   16. ○ A ○ B ○ C ○ D ○ E

4. ○ A ○ B ○ C ○ D ○ E   17. ○ A ○ B ○ C ○ D ○ E

5. ○ A ○ B ○ C ○ D ○ E   18. ○ A ○ B ○ C ○ D ○ E

6. ○ A ○ B ○ C ○ D ○ E   19. ○ A ○ B ○ C ○ D ○ E

7. ○ A ○ B ○ C ○ D ○ E   20. ○ A ○ B ○ C ○ D ○ E

8. ○ A ○ B ○ C ○ D ○ E   21. ○ A ○ B ○ C ○ D ○ E

9. ○ A ○ B ○ C ○ D ○ E   22. ○ A ○ B ○ C ○ D ○ E

10. ○ A ○ B ○ C ○ D ○ E   23. ○ A ○ B ○ C ○ D ○ E

11. ○ A ○ B ○ C ○ D ○ E   24. ○ A ○ B ○ C ○ D ○ E

12. ○ A ○ B ○ C ○ D ○ E   25. ○ A ○ B ○ C ○ D ○ E

13. ○ A ○ B ○ C ○ D ○ E

Methods and Measurement

KEY TO PRACTICE TEST

1. D
2. B
3. B
4. A
5. E
6. C
7. D
8. C
9. C
10. B
11. D
12. E
13. E
14. D
15. D
16. D
17. D
18. E
19. D
20. B
21. A
22. D
23. B
24. B
25. A

Section II: Physical Science

LESSONS AND ACTIVITIES

Lesson 13 Students will build a simple series circuit using wires, batteries, bulbs, and a switch. They will observe what happens when additional bulbs are added to the circuit.

Lesson 14 Students will build a simple series circuit using wires, batteries, bulbs, and a switch. They will observe what happens when additional batteries are added to the circuit.

Lesson 15 Students will build a simple parallel circuit using wires, batteries, bulbs, and a switch.

Lesson 16 Students will show how the Earth's magnetic field can be detected by a magnet.

Lesson 17 Students will make a simple magnet.

Lesson 18 Students will make a simple compass to detect the presence of the Earth's magnetic field.

Lesson 19 Students will show that electric currents produce magnetic fields.

Lesson 20 Students will build a simple electromagnet.

Lesson 21 Students will build a simple electric motor to show how electrical energy can be changed to motion.

Lesson 22 Students will examine a circuit used to make a doorbell ring.

Lesson 23 Students will construct an electroscope to show that electrically charged objects repel each other.

Lesson 24 Students will show that electrically charged objects repel each other.

Lesson 25 Students will show that magnets have two poles.

Lesson 26 Students will show that the like poles of two magnets repel each other while unlike poles attract.

Lesson 27 Students will draw the magnetic field lines around a bar magnet to illustrate the force fields surrounding it.

Lesson 28 Students will demonstrate that electrical energy is quickly changed to heat energy.

Lesson 29 Students will build a lightbulb to show how electrical energy is changed to light energy.

Lesson 30 Students will build a battery to show how chemical energy is changed to electrical energy.

PHYSICAL SCIENCE PRACTICE TEST

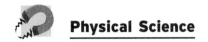

Lesson 13: Teacher Preparation

Basic Principle   Electricity and magnetism are related effects that have many useful applications in daily life.

Competency   Students will build a simple series circuit using wires, batteries, bulbs, and a switch. They will observe what happens when additional appliances (e.g., a second bulb) are added to a circuit powered by a single battery.

Materials   thin-gauge insulated copper wire, alligator clips, standard D-cell batteries with holders, small lightbulbs with standard sockets, switches

Procedure   Prepare for the lesson by stripping the insulation off the ends of 4-inch to 6-inch lengths of thin-gauge insulated copper wire. Connect alligator clips to the bare ends of each section of wire. Insert appropriate flashlight bulbs into their sockets. MAKE SURE ALL SWITCHES ARE IN THE "OPEN" POSITION. Place D-cell batteries in battery holders that facilitate clip connections. Assist students in constructing the circuits shown in Figure A and Figure B of this TEACHER PREPARATION guide and on STUDENT HANDOUT—LESSON 13. Give them time to test their circuits and answer the questions as directed.

Observations & Analysis

- *Answer to question 1:* The bulb lights because electricity flows through a closed circuit. The electrical energy flowing through the circuit heats up the filament inside the bulb, causing it to give off light and heat.
- *Answer to question 2:* The bulbs are dimmer because they are sharing the electrical energy supplied by a single battery.
- *Answer to question 3:* Both bulbs go out because the circuit is broken. Unscrewing either bulb stops the flow of electricity through the circuit.

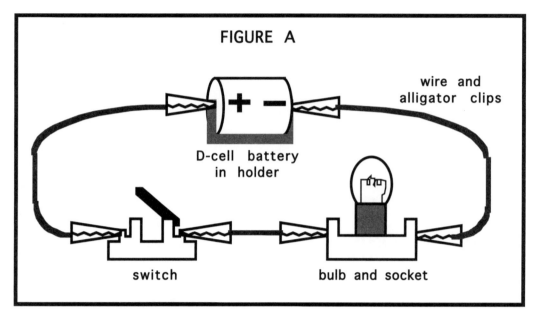

FIGURE A

wire and
alligator clips

D-cell battery
in holder

switch

bulb and socket

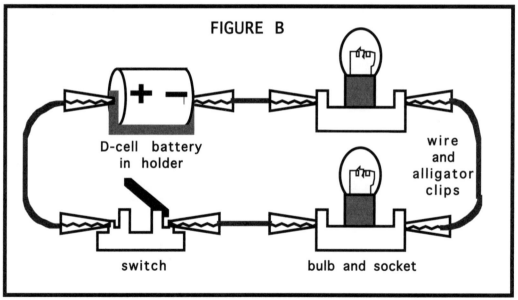

FIGURE B

D-cell battery
in holder

wire
and
alligator
clips

switch

bulb and socket

Name _____ **Date** _____

Physical Science

STUDENT HANDOUT–LESSON 13

Basic Principle Electricity and magnetism are related effects that have many useful applications in daily life.

Objective Build a simple series circuit using wires, batteries, bulbs, and a switch. Observe what happens when additional bulbs are added to the circuit.

Materials thin-gauge insulated copper wire, alligator clips, standard D-cell batteries with holders, small lightbulbs with standard sockets, switch

Procedure READ EACH STEP ONE SENTENCE AT A TIME.

1. Refer to Figure A. Connect one wire by a clip to the minus (–) side of the battery. This wire can be called the *negative wire*.

2. Connect the loose clip on the negative wire to one side of the bulb and socket.

3. Connect the clip of another loose wire to the other side of the socket.

4. Connect the clip of the loose wire attached to the socket to one side of an OPEN SWITCH. Make sure the switch is open!

5. Connect the clip of another loose wire to the other side of the open switch.

6. Connect this wire to the plus (+) side of the battery. This wire can be called the *positive wire*.

7. Close the switch. Observe what happens. Open the switch and answer the first question.

8. MAKE SURE YOUR SWITCH IS OPEN. Add a second bulb to the circuit as shown in Figure B.

9. Close the switch. Observe what happens. Open the switch and answer the second question.

10. Close the switch. Unscrew one of the bulbs. Observe what happens and answer the third question.

Observations & Analysis

1. Why does the bulb light up when you close the switch?

   _____

   _____

2. How bright are the two bulbs? Compare their brightness with the single bulb in the first circuit you built. Explain your observation.

   _____

   _____

3. What happened when you unscrewed one of the bulbs? Explain why this happened.

   _____

   _____

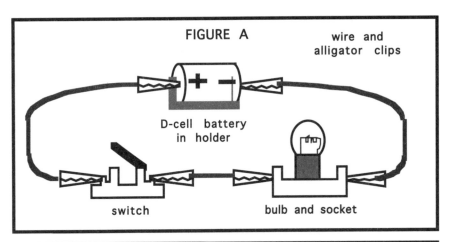

FIGURE A

wire and alligator clips

D-cell battery in holder

switch

bulb and socket

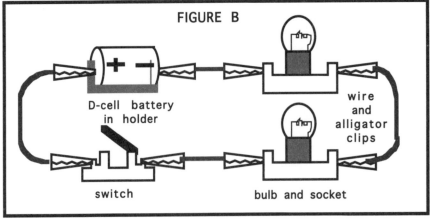

FIGURE B

D-cell battery in holder

wire and alligator clips

switch

bulb and socket

Lesson 14: Teacher Preparation

Basic Principle   Electricity and magnetism are related effects that have many useful applications in daily life.

Competency   Students will build a simple series circuit using wires, batteries, bulbs, and a switch. They will observe what happens when the circuit is supplied with additional power (e.g., a second battery).

Materials   thin-gauge insulated copper wire, alligator clips, standard D-cell batteries with holders, small lightbulbs with standard sockets, switches

Procedure   Prepare for the lesson as you did in LESSON 13. Strip the insulation off the ends of 4-inch to 6-inch lengths of thin-gauge insulated copper wire. Connect alligator clips to the bare ends of each section of wire. Insert appropriate flashlight bulbs into their sockets. MAKE SURE ALL SWITCHES ARE IN THE "OPEN" POSITION. Place D-cell batteries in battery holders that facilitate clip connections. Assist students in constructing the circuits shown in Figure A, Figure B, and Figure C of this TEACHER PREPARATION guide and on STUDENT HANDOUT—LESSON 14. Give them time to test their circuits and answer the questions as directed.

Observations & Analysis

- *Answer to question 1:* This review question should have the same answer as that of the first question in Lesson 13. The bulb lights because electricity flows through a closed circuit. The electrical energy flowing through the circuit heats up the filament inside the bulb, causing it to give off light and heat.

- *Answer to question 2:* The bulb is brighter because the added battery supplies additional electrical energy to the circuit.

- *Answer to question 3:* The bulbs are dimmer because they must share the electrical energy supplied by the batteries.

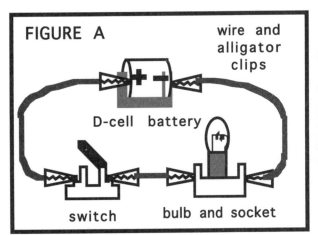

FIGURE A

wire and alligator clips

D-cell battery

switch

bulb and socket

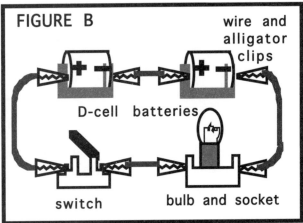

FIGURE B

wire and alligator clips

D-cell batteries

switch

bulb and socket

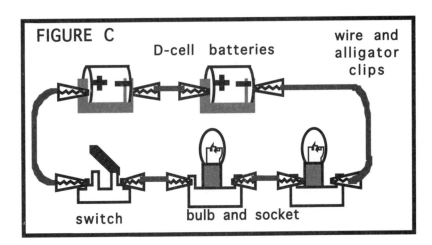

FIGURE C

D-cell batteries

wire and alligator clips

switch

bulb and socket

Physical Science

STUDENT HANDOUT–LESSON 14

Basic Principle   Electricity and magnetism are related effects that have many useful applications in daily life.

Objective   Build a simple series circuit using wires, batteries, bulbs, and a switch. Observe what happens when additional batteries are added to the circuit.

Materials   thin-gauge insulated copper wire, alligator clips, standard D-cell batteries with holders, small lightbulbs with standard sockets, switch

Procedure   READ EACH STEP ONE SENTENCE AT A TIME.

1. Refer to Figure A. Connect one wire by a clip to the minus (–) side of the battery. This wire can be called the *negative wire*.

2. Connect the loose clip on the negative wire to one side of the bulb and socket.

3. Connect the clip of another loose wire to the other side of the socket.

4. Connect the clip of the loose wire attached to the socket to one side of an OPEN SWITCH. Make sure the switch is open!

5. Connect the clip of another loose wire to the other side of the open switch.

6. Connect this wire to the plus (+) side of the battery. This wire can be called the *positive wire*.

7. Close the switch. Observe what happens. Open the switch and answer the first question.

8. MAKE SURE YOUR SWITCH IS OPEN. Add a second battery to the circuit as shown in Figure B.

9. Close the switch. Observe what happens. Open the switch and answer the second question.

10. MAKE SURE YOUR SWITCH IS OPEN. Add a second bulb to the circuit as shown in Figure C.

11. Close the switch. Observe what happens. Open the switch and answer the third question.

Observations & Analysis

1. Why does the bulb light up when you close the switch?

   _____

   _____

2. How bright is the bulb? Compare its brightness with the bulb in the first circuit you built. Explain your observation.

   _____

   _____

3. How bright are the two bulbs? Compare their brightness with the bulb in the first and second circuits you built. Explain your observation.

   _____

   _____

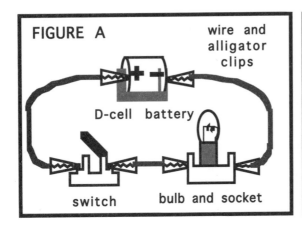

FIGURE A — wire and alligator clips — D-cell battery — switch — bulb and socket

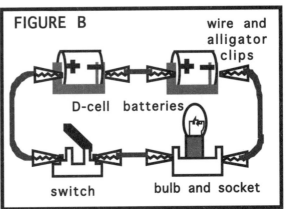

FIGURE B — wire and alligator clips — D-cell batteries — switch — bulb and socket

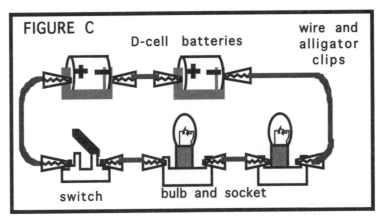

FIGURE C — D-cell batteries — wire and alligator clips — switch — bulb and socket

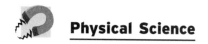

Lesson 15: Teacher Preparation

Basic Principle   Electricity and magnetism are related effects that have many useful applications in daily life.

Competency   Students will build a simple parallel circuit using wires, batteries, bulbs, and a switch.

Materials   thin-gauge insulated copper wire, alligator clips, standard D-cell batteries with holders, small lightbulbs with standard sockets, switches

Procedure   Prepare for the lesson as you did in LESSON 13 and LESSON 14. Strip the insulation off the ends of 4-inch to 6-inch lengths of thin-gauge insulated copper wire. Connect alligator clips to the bare ends of each section of wire. Insert appropriate flashlight bulbs into their sockets. MAKE SURE ALL SWITCHES ARE IN THE "OPEN" POSITION. Place D-cell batteries in battery holders that facilitate clip connections. Assist students in constructing the circuits shown in Figure A and Figure B of this TEACHER PREPARATION guide and on STUDENT HANDOUT—LESSON 15. Give them time to test their circuits and answer the questions as directed.

Observations & Analysis

- *Answer to question 1:* The bulbs light because electricity flows through a closed circuit. The electrical energy flowing through the circuit heats up the filaments inside the bulbs, causing them to give off light and heat. Students should draw an arrow starting at the negative side of the battery through the circuit. The arrows should illustrate the "splitting" flow of electricity through the alligator clips, bulbs, and wires, showing more than one pathway leading back to the positive side of the battery.

- *Answer to question 2:* The second bulb remains lit because the electricity can flow through more than one path.

- *Answer to question 3:* The bulbs are brighter because the circuit has been supplied with additional electrical energy.

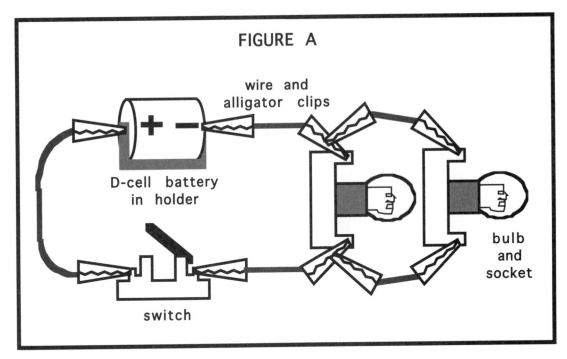

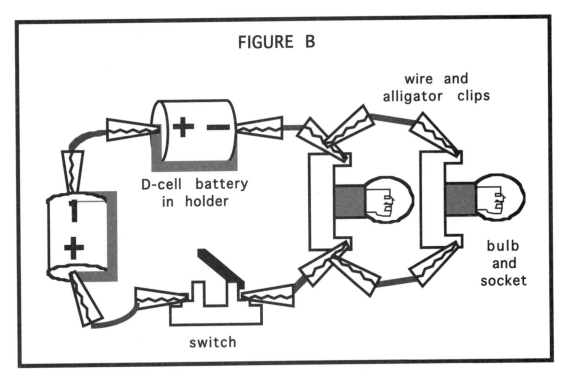

Physical Science

STUDENT HANDOUT–LESSON 15

Basic Principle   Electricity and magnetism are related effects that have many useful applications in daily life.

Objective   Build a simple parallel circuit using wires, batteries, bulbs, and a switch.

Materials   thin-gauge insulated copper wire, alligator clips, standard D-cell batteries with holders, small lightbulbs with standard sockets, switch

Procedure   READ EACH STEP ONE SENTENCE AT A TIME.

1. Refer to Figure A. Connect one wire by a clip to the minus (–) side of the battery. This wire can be called the *negative wire.*

2. Connect the loose clip on the negative wire to one side of the bulb and socket.

3. Connect the clip of another loose wire to the other side of the socket.

4. Connect the clip of the loose wire attached to the socket to one side of an OPEN SWITCH. Make sure the switch is open!

5. Connect the clip of another loose wire to the other side of the open switch.

6. Connect this wire to the plus (+) side of the battery. This wire can be called the *positive wire.*

7. Connect two wires by their clips to the sides of a second bulb and socket.

8. Connect the clips of these wires to the clips attached to the first bulb and socket.

9. Close the switch. Observe what happens. Open the switch. Answer the first question.

10. Close the switch and unscrew one of the bulbs. Observe what happens. Open the switch. Answer the second question.

11. Add a second battery to the circuit as shown in Figure B. Close the switch. Observe what happens. Open the switch. Answer the third question.

Observations & Analysis

1. Why do the bulbs light up when you close the switch? Draw arrows in Figure A to show how the current can flow through different paths.

   _____

   _____

2. What happens when you unscrew one of the bulbs from its socket? Explain your observation.

   _____

   _____

3. How bright are the two bulbs? Compare their brightness with the bulbs in the first circuit you built. Explain your observation.

   _____

   _____

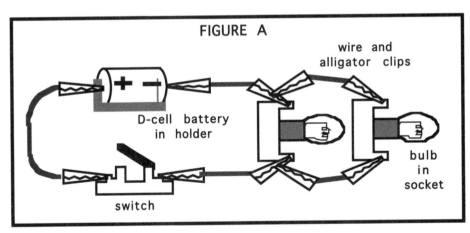

FIGURE A

wire and alligator clips

D-cell battery in holder

switch

bulb in socket

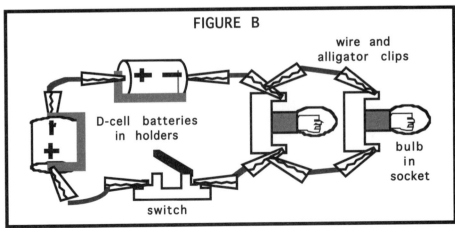

FIGURE B

wire and alligator clips

D-cell batteries in holders

switch

bulb in socket

Lesson 16: Teacher Preparation

Basic Principle   Electricity and magnetism are related effects that have many useful applications in daily life.

Competency   Students will show how the Earth's magnetic field can be detected by a bar magnet.

Materials   compass, string, bar magnet, tape

Procedure

1. Demonstrate the use of a magnetic compass. Explain that the needle of a magnetic compass is a simple magnet made with materials such as <u>a</u>luminum, <u>ni</u>ckel, or <u>co</u>balt. A mixture of these three metals produces an alloy called <u>alnico</u> that has magnetic properties. Show students how to align the compass needle, pointing to the North Pole of Earth, with the letter "N" on the compass.

2. Demonstrate how to identify the other directions using the northern direction as the reference direction. Assist students in following the Procedure given on STU-DENT HANDOUT—LESSON 16. Give them time to make their observations and answer the questions as directed.

Observations & Analysis

- Students should draw the hanging bar magnet pointing in the same direction as the compass needle.

- *Answer to question 2:* Yes. The hanging bar magnet pointed in the same direction as the compass needle.

- *Answer to question 3:* The Earth must be surrounded by an invisible field of magnetism. This invisible magnetic field must flow in the same direction as the magnetic fields surrounding the compass needle and the bar magnet.

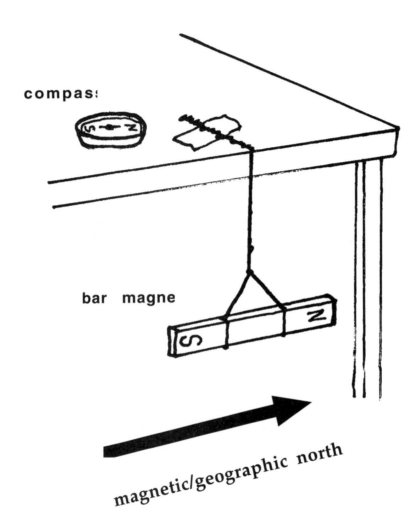

compass

bar magnet

magnetic/geographic north

Name _____ **Date** _____

Physical Science
STUDENT HANDOUT–LESSON 16

Basic Principle   Electricity and magnetism are related effects that have many useful applications in daily life.

Objective   Show how the Earth's magnetic field can be detected by a magnet.

Materials   compass, string, bar magnet, tape

Procedure   READ EACH STEP ONE SENTENCE AT A TIME.

1. Tie a string around a bar magnet as shown.

2. Hang the magnet over the edge of a table. Tape the string in place and allow the magnet to swing freely until it comes to rest.

3. Place the compass on the table near the string.

4. Compare the directions of the bar magnet and the compass needle.

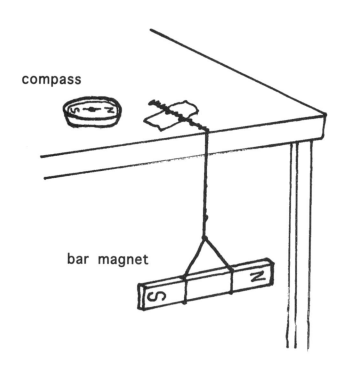

Observations & Analysis

1. Draw your observations.

2. Did the bar magnet point in the same direction as the compass needle?

   _____

   _____

3. Explain your observations.

   _____

   _____

   _____

   _____

Lesson 17: Teacher Preparation

Basic Principle   Electricity and magnetism are related effects that have many useful applications in daily life.

Competency   Students will show how to make a simple magnet.

Materials   sewing needle or paper clip, magnet, iron filings, paper towel

Procedure

1. Inform students that magnetism is created by electrons. Explain that electrons are among the tiniest electrical particles found inside atoms. Add that atoms are the invisible particles that make up the matter all around us. Explain that every electron spins wildly on its axis, much like the Earth rotates on its axis. Draw Illustration A to illustrate this point. As the electron spins, it creates a force called *electromagnetism*. While electrons are usually flying around inside atoms in many different directions, they sometimes line up and spin in the same direction. When they do this, their combined electromagnetic fields all flow in the same direction. A bar of metal whose trillions of electrons all spin in the same direction becomes surrounded by a magnetic field.

2. Explain that a rock called *lodestone* is a natural magnet made of the elements iron and oxygen. Manmade magnets are made of a variety of different metal alloys.

3. Explain that stroking a natural or manmade magnet along a metal needle, paper clip, or pin forces the electrons in those metals to line up like those in the magnet. Draw Illustration B to compare the electron arrangement in a normal piece of metal with that of the electron arrangement in a magnetized piece of metal. Assist students in following the Procedure given on STUDENT HANDOUT—LESSON 17. Give them time to make their observations and answer the questions as directed.

Observations & Analysis

- Students should draw the iron filings sticking to their new magnet.

- *Answer to the question:* Students should explain that stroking the needle with the bar magnet caused the electrons inside the atoms of the needle or paper clip to line up and spin the same direction.

ILLUSTRATION A

An electron spinning on its axis creates an electromagnetic field

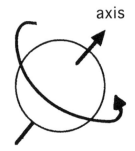

axis

ILLUSTRATION B

normal piece of metal	**magnetized piece of metal**

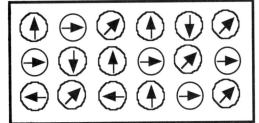
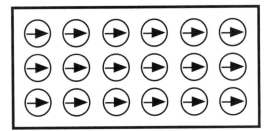

electrons spinning
in many different directions

electrons spinning
in the same direction

---

stroke in only
one direction

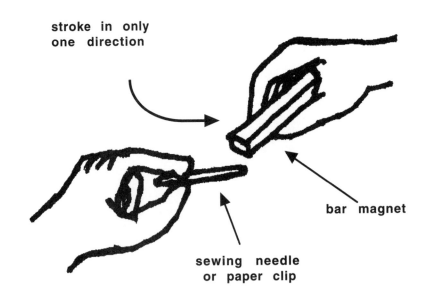

bar magnet

sewing needle
or paper clip

Name _____ **Date** _____

Physical Science

STUDENT HANDOUT–LESSON 17

Basic Principle   Electricity and magnetism are related effects that have many useful applications in daily life.

Objective   Make a simple magnet.

Materials   sewing needle or paper clip, magnet, iron filings, paper towel

Procedure   READ EACH STEP ONE SENTENCE AT A TIME.

1. Pour a small pile of iron filings onto a paper towel.

2. Stroke a sewing needle or paper clip with a bar magnet in one direction as shown.

3. Touch the needle or paper clip to the small pile of iron filings.

4. Record your observations.

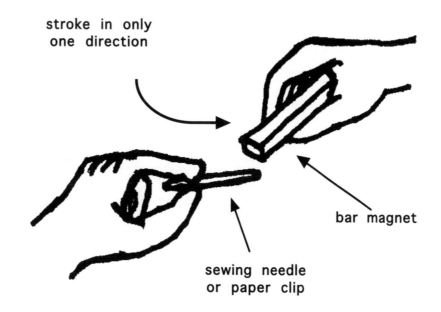

stroke in only
one direction

bar magnet

sewing needle
or paper clip

Observations & Analysis   Draw your observations.

Explain your observations.

_____

_____

_____

_____

_____

_____

_____

_____

_____

_____

_____

_____

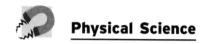

Lesson 18: Teacher Preparation

Basic Principle   Electricity and magnetism are related effects that have many useful applications in daily life.

Competency   Students will show how to make a simple compass.

Materials   compass, sewing needle or paper clip, magnet, sponge, bowl, water

Procedure   The Chinese scientist Shen Kua invented a magnetic compass much like the one in this lesson around 1088 A.D. A compass always points North, aligning itself with the magnetic field created by the Earth's rotating core of iron and nickel. Draw Illustration A to show students the orientation of the Earth's magnetic field as it spins on its axis from West to East. Assist students in following the Procedure given on STUDENT HANDOUT—LESSON 18. Give them time to make their observations and answer the questions as directed.

Observations & Analysis

- Students should draw the magnetized needle on the floating sponge pointing in the same direction as the compass needle.
- *Answer to question 2:* Yes. The magnetized needle on the floating sponge pointed in the same direction as the compass needle that pointed toward the North Pole.
- *Answer to question 3:* The magnetized needle lined up with the Earth's magnetic field.

ILLUSTRATION A

The iron-nickel core of the Earth rotates on its axis, creating a magnetic field that encircles the planet from pole to pole.

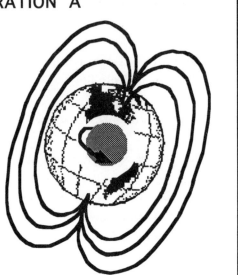

stroke in only one direction

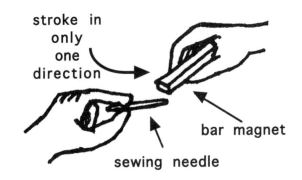

bar magnet

sewing needle

Name _____ **Date** _____

Physical Science
STUDENT HANDOUT–LESSON 18

Basic Principle   Electricity and magnetism are related effects that have many useful applications in daily life.

Objective   Make a simple compass to detect the presence of the Earth's magnetic field.

Materials   compass, sewing needle or paper clip, magnet, sponge, bowl, water

Procedure   READ EACH STEP ONE SENTENCE AT A TIME.

1. Stroke a sewing needle or paper clip with a bar magnet in one direction as shown. This will cause the needle to become a weak magnet for several minutes.

2. Fill a bowl with water.

3. Float a small piece of sponge in the bowl.

4. Carefully place the needle in the center of the sponge.

5. Wait a minute. Then note the direction of the needle.

6. Place the compass next to the bowl.

7. Compare the directions of the needle on the sponge and the compass needle.

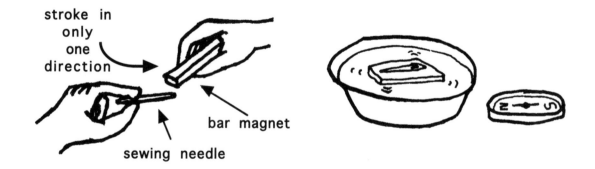

stroke in only one direction

bar magnet

sewing needle

Observations & Analysis

1. Draw your observations.

2. Did the needle in the bowl point in the same direction as the compass needle?

   _____

   _____

3. Explain your observations.

   _____

   _____

   _____

   _____

   _____

   _____

 **Physical Science**

Lesson 19: Teacher Preparation

Basic Principle   Electricity and magnetism are related effects that have many useful applications in daily life.

Competency   Students will show that electric currents produce magnetic fields.

Materials   compass, battery, thin-gauge insulated wire, switch

Procedure

1. Prepare for the lesson by stripping the insulation off the ends of 4-inch to 6-inch lengths of thin-gauge insulated copper wire. Connect alligator clips to the bare ends of each section of wire. Make sure all switches are in the "open" position. Place D-cell batteries in battery holders that facilitate clip connections. The Danish scientist Hans Christian Oersted (1777–1851) discovered in 1820 that an electric current produces a magnetic field. He was demonstrating the properties of an electric current to his students when a compass needle near the wires he was using began to change direction. This discovery was the beginning of a new era in science and technology. The English scientist Michael Faraday (1791–1867) used Oersted's discovery to invent the transformer, a device used to increase or decrease the strength of an electric current. These breakthroughs allowed other inventors to invent many devices that help us to do work with electricity.

2. Assist students in constructing the circuits shown in the drawing here and on STUDENT HANDOUT—LESSON 18. Give them time to test their circuits and answer the questions as directed.

Observations & Analysis

- Students should draw the compass needle pointing at a right angle to the flow of current moving through the insulated wire.

- *Answer to question 2:* The compass needle changed position and pointed away from the wire when the switch was closed.

- *Answer to question 3:* The current flowing through the wire must create a magnetic field much like the magnetic field of Earth. This manmade field caused the compass to change position.

BEFORE THE CURRENT IS FLOWING

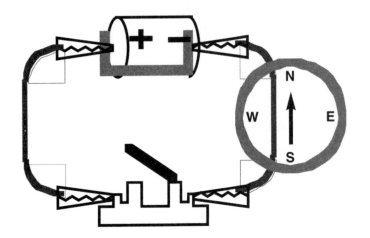

When the electricity is not flowing through the circuit, the compass needle will align with the wire as long as the wire is pointing north.

AFTER THE CURRENT IS FLOWING

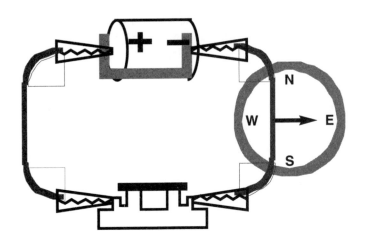

When the electricity is flowing through the circuit, the compass needle points at a right angle to the flow of current. This allows us to conclude that an electric current generates a magnetic field that is perpendicular to the flow of electricity.

Name _____ **Date** _____

Physical Science

STUDENT HANDOUT–LESSON 19

Basic Principle Electricity and magnetism are related effects that have many useful applications in daily life.

Objective Show that electric currents produce magnetic fields.

Materials compass, battery, thin-gauge insulated wire, switch

Procedure READ EACH STEP ONE SENTENCE AT A TIME.

1. Build the electric circuit shown. MAKE SURE THE SWITCH STAYS OPEN.

2. Place the compass under a section of wire. Line up the wire with the compass needle so that both point north.

3. Close the switch and note the new position of the compass needle.

4. Open the switch and record your observations.

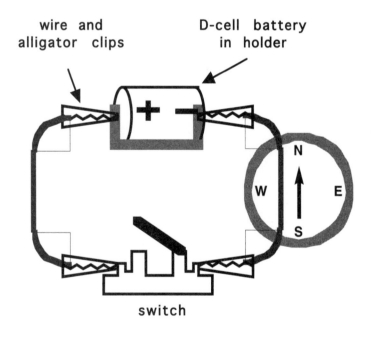

Observations & Analysis

1. Draw your observations.

2. What happened to the compass needle when you closed the switch?

_____

_____

_____

_____

_____

_____

3. Explain your observations.

_____

_____

_____

_____

_____

_____

_____

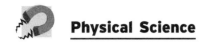

Lesson 20: Teacher Preparation

Basic Principle   Electricity and magnetism are related effects that have many useful applications in daily life.

Competency   Students will build a simple electromagnet.

Materials   battery, thin-gauge insulated wire, switch, iron nail, iron filings and paper clips, paper towel

Procedure

1. Prepare for the lesson as you did in previous circuitry lessons by stripping the insulation off the ends of 4-inch to 6-inch lengths of thin-gauge insulated copper wire. Connect alligator clips to the bare ends of each section of wire. Make sure all switches are in the "open" position. Place D-cell batteries in battery holders that facilitate clip connections. The English scientist William Sturgeon (1783–1850) invented the first electromagnet in 1823. The American scientist Joseph Henry (1797–1878) insulated his wires with silk and built electromagnets capable of lifting objects more than 2,000 pounds heavier than the magnet itself!

2. Assist students in constructing the circuits shown in the drawing here and on STUDENT HANDOUT—LESSON 20. Give them time to test their circuits and answer the questions as directed.

Observations & Analysis

- Students should draw the iron filings and paper clips sticking to their electromagnet when the switch is closed and the current is flowing.

- *Answer to question 2:* The iron filings and paper clips stuck to the electromagnet when the switch was closed.

- *Answer to question 3:* The paper clips that stick to the electromagnet can attract iron filings and other paper clips when the current is flowing.

- *Answer to question 4:* The current flowing through the wire creates a magnetic field that causes the iron nail to become magnetized.

COMPLETE ELECTROMAGNET

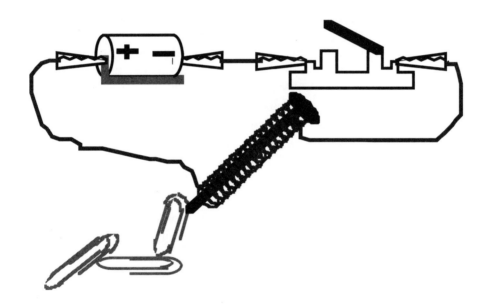

Physical Science
STUDENT HANDOUT–LESSON 20

Basic Principle   Electricity and magnetism are related effects that have many useful applications in daily life.

Objective   Build a simple electromagnet.

Materials   battery, thin-gauge insulated wire, switch, iron nail, iron filings and paper clips, paper towel

Procedure   READ EACH STEP ONE SENTENCE AT A TIME.

1. Neatly coil a length of thin-gauge insulated wire around a clean iron nail. DO NOT CRISSCROSS OR CHANGE THE DIRECTION OF THE WIRE AS YOU WRAP IT AROUND THE NAIL.

2. Build the electric circuit shown. MAKE SURE THE SWITCH STAYS OPEN.

3. Pour some iron filings and place several paper clips on a paper towel.

4. Close the switch and place either end of the nail near the filings and clips. Observe what happens.

5. Open the switch and record your observations.

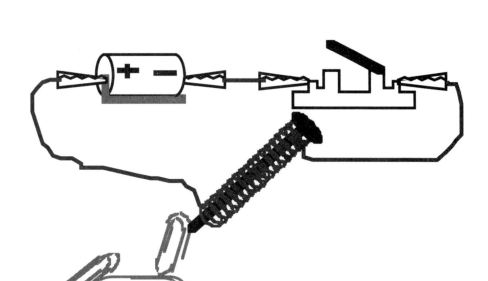

Observations & Analysis

1. Draw your observations.

2. What happened to the iron filings and paper clips when you closed the switch?

   _____

   _____

3. What observations show that the clips also become magnetized when they are attached to the electromagnet?

   _____

   _____

4. Explain your observations.

   _____

   _____

   _____

   _____

   _____

   _____

   _____

 **Physical Science**

Lesson 21: Teacher Preparation

Basic Principle   Electricity and magnetism are related effects that have many useful applications in daily life.

Competency   Students will build a simple motor to show how electrical energy can be changed to motion.

Materials   battery, thin-gauge insulated wire, switch, iron nails, cardboard, large paper clips, masking or electrical tape, nail polish, bar magnet

Procedure

1. Find the appropriate lengths of wire required to construct the electromagnets used in this lesson by coiling a length of thin-gauge insulated wire around two iron nails taped together. Refer to the illustration here and on STUDENT HAND-OUT—LESSON 21. Strip about 1 inch of insulation off the ends of each length of wire. Paint the top half of one bare end with nail polish and allow the polish to dry. Leave the other end completely bare. The dry polish will serve as insulation that intermittently stops the flow of current as the electromagnet spins on its axis. Cut small pieces of cardboard about 2 inches square. Connect alligator clips to the bare ends of 4-inch to 6-inch sections of circuitry wire as done in previous lessons. Make sure all switches are in the "open" position. Place D-cell batteries in battery holders that facilitate clip connections.

2. The English scientist Michael Faraday (1791–1867) invented the first electric motor in 1821 by placing a current-carrying wire between the poles of two magnets. The opposing magnetic fields caused the wire to rotate. This is the basic principle of a motor.

3. Assist students in constructing the electromagnet, motor, and circuit shown in the drawing here and on STUDENT HANDOUT—LESSON 21. Give them time to test their circuits and answer the question as directed.

Observations & Analysis   Students' answers will vary, but should show some thought reflecting their understanding of the basic principle of the device.

BUILDING A SIMPLE MOTOR

Step 1: Construct electromagnets by coiling thin-gauge insulated wire around two taped iron nails. You should end with about 2 inches of wire at each end. One end is bare. One side of the other end is insulated with dry nail polish.

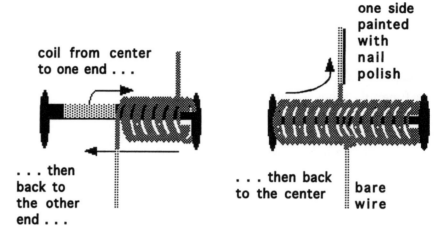

coil from center to one end . . .

. . . then back to the other end . . .

one side painted with nail polish

. . . then back to the center

bare wire

Step 2: Bend two large paper clips and insert them into the slots of a square piece of cardboard.

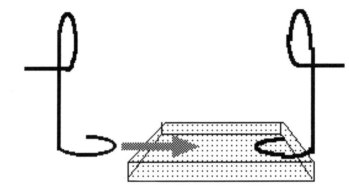

Step 3: Thread the wires of the electromagnet through the "eyes" of the paper clips. Balance the magnet so that it spins freely on its axis. Complete the electric circuit and place one pole of a bar magnet under the nail.

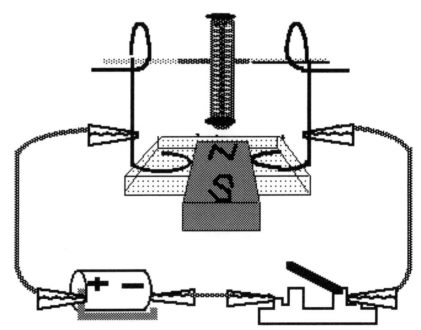

Physical Science
STUDENT HANDOUT–LESSON 21

Basic Principle   Electricity and magnetism are related effects that have many useful applications in daily life.

Objective   Build a simple electric motor to show how electrical energy can be changed to motion.

Materials   battery, thin-gauge insulated wire, switch, two iron nails, cardboard square, large paper clip, masking or electrical tape, colored nail polish, bar magnet

Procedure   READ EACH STEP ONE SENTENCE AT A TIME.

1. Tape two iron nails together with masking or electrical tape. Build a simple electromagnet by coiling thin-gauge insulated wire around the two taped nails as shown. Begin coiling at the center of the nails leaving about 2 inches of wire at the end. DO NOT CHANGE DIRECTION AS YOU COVER THE NAILS. WIND THE WIRE IN ONE CONTINUOUS COIL FROM NAIL HEAD TO NAIL HEAD. When you are done, you will have a "double layer" of wire surrounding the nails. One end of the wire is bare. The other end is coated on one side with dry nail polish. The spinning electromagnet of a motor is called the *armature*.

2. Bend two large paper clips into the shapes shown. Insert the clips into the "slots" inside a piece of square cardboard. This device will serve as the stand for the armature.

3. Thread the wires of the electromagnet through the "eyes" of the bent paper clips. Position the ends of the wires so that the magnet can spin freely between the clips.

4. Complete the electric circuit shown. KEEP THE SWITCH OPEN.

5. Position one end of a bar magnet under the electromagnet.

6. Close the switch and give the electromagnet a spin. Adjust the position of the bar magnet until the electromagnet spins freely under its own power. OPEN THE SWITCH IMMEDIATELY IF THE WIRE BEGINS TO HEAT.

THE ELECTROMAGNET

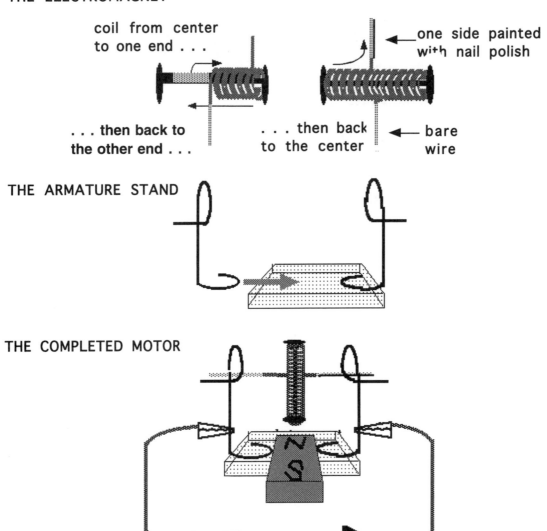

coil from center
to one end . . .

one side painted
with nail polish

. . . then back to
the other end . . .

. . . then back
to the center

bare
wire

THE ARMATURE STAND

THE COMPLETED MOTOR

Observations & Analysis Suggest ways to improve the design of this electric motor.

_____

_____

_____

_____

 **Physical Science**

Lesson 22: Teacher Preparation

Basic Principle   Electricity and magnetism are related effects that have many useful applications in daily life.

Competency   Students will examine the circuit used to make a doorbell ring.

Observations & Analysis   Assist students in tracing the pathway of current from the negative side of the battery, through the switch, wires, electromagnet, and metal conductors of the circuit, back to the positive side of the battery. Refer to the diagram shown here. Students should note that the current flowing through the electromagnet is interrupted when the metal striker that rings the bell is drawn away from the metal breaker completing the circuit. When the electromagnet is turned off by the break in the circuit, the metal striker springs back into position against the metal breaker completing the circuit. The electromagnet is activated again by the renewed flow of current, causing the cycle to repeat.

FLOW OF CURRENT THROUGH A DOORBELL

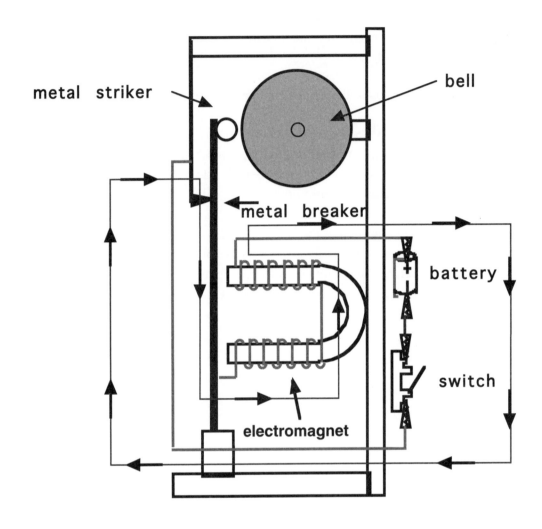

metal striker

bell

metal breaker

battery

electromagnet

switch

Name _____ **Date** _____

Physical Science

STUDENT HANDOUT–LESSON 22

Basic Principle   Electricity and magnetism are related effects that have many useful applications in daily life.

Objective   Examine a circuit used to make a doorbell ring.

Study the Diagram   The picture shown below is a diagram of an electric circuit used to make a doorbell ring. The electric current can pass through the gray wire and both the metal breaker and metal striker. Describe what will happen when the switch is closed in *Observation & Analysis*.

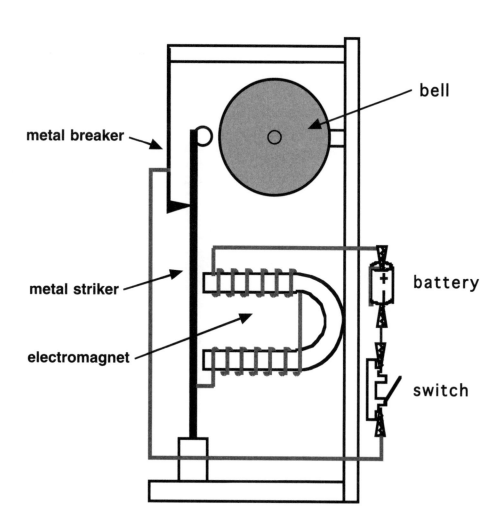

Observations & Analysis

_____

_____

_____

_____

_____

_____

_____

_____

_____

_____

_____

 **Physical Science**

Lesson 23: Teacher Preparation

Basic Principle   Electricity and magnetism are related effects that have many useful applications in daily life.

Competency   Students will construct an electroscope to show that electrically charged objects repel each other.

Materials   Ehrlenmeyer flask, one-holed rubber stopper, iron nail, sharp pencil, aluminum foil, uninsulated thin-gauge wire, balloon, wool or silk cloth

Procedure   Prepare for the lesson by uncoiling strands of iron picture-hanging wire to separate the thin metal threads. Students will use the thin metal threads to construct the electroscope in this lesson. Draw Illustration A to show how a balloon becomes coated with electrical particles after it is rubbed with wool or silk. These particles are electrons, the tiny negatively charged particles that are found inside the atoms that make up all matter. Help students to safely insert the nail into the rubber stopper as instructed in Step 2 on their handout. Assist them in following the Procedure given on STUDENT HANDOUT—LESSON 23. Give them time to make their observations and answer the questions as directed.

Observations & Analysis

- Students should draw the aluminum foil strips moving apart as the charged balloon moves closer to the nail.

- *Answer to the question:* Students should observe that electrical charges on the balloon (i.e., the electrons) have moved to the nail and down to the aluminum strips. They should conclude that the electrical particles coating the strips of foil all have the same electrical charge and that these charges repel one another.

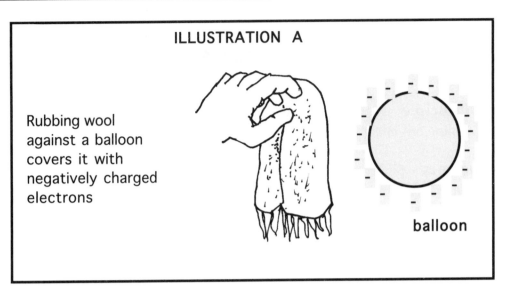

ILLUSTRATION A

Rubbing wool against a balloon covers it with negatively charged electrons

balloon

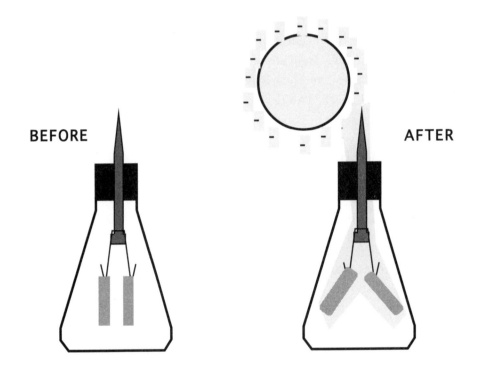

BEFORE

AFTER

Physical Science
STUDENT HANDOUT–LESSON 23

Basic Principle   Electricity and magnetism are related effects that have many useful applications in daily life.

Objective   Construct an electroscope to show that electrically charged objects repel each other.

Materials   Ehrlenmeyer flask, one-holed rubber stopper, iron nail, sharp pencil, aluminum foil, uninsulated thin-gauge wire, balloon, wool or silk cloth

Procedure   READ EACH STEP ONE SENTENCE AT A TIME.

1. Wrap a section of uninsulated thin-gauge metal wire around the head of an iron nail.

2. Carefully insert the nail through the hole of a one-holed rubber stopper.

3. Cut two small rectangular strips of thin aluminum foil and rub the foil flat. AVOID TEARING THE FOIL.

4. Use a sharp pencil to carefully punch a small hole in the end of each piece of foil.

5. Hang each piece of foil loosely from the ends of the wire.

6. Carefully insert the aluminum strips into an Ehrlenmeyer flask and plug the flask as shown. Be careful not to damage the aluminum strips.

7. Inflate a balloon and rub it with wool or silk cloth.

8. Place the balloon near the point of the nail.

9. Record you observations.

AN ELECTROSCOPE

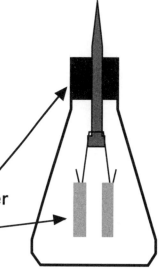

nail and rubber stopper

aluminum foil strips

Observations & Analysis

1. Draw what happened when you touched the charged balloon to the point of the nail.

2. Explain your observations.

_____

_____

_____

_____

_____

_____

_____

_____

_____

_____

_____

_____

 **Physical Science**

Lesson 24: Teacher Preparation

Basic Principle   Electricity and magnetism are related effects that have many useful applications in daily life.

Competency   Students will show that electrically charged objects repel each other.

Materials   string, tape, balloons, wool or silk cloth

Procedure   This lesson demonstrates the same principle learned in LESSON 23. Electrically charged objects having the same electrical charge repel one another. Since both balloons in this activity are treated in the same manner (i.e., they are both rubbed with the same kind of cloth), they must be coated with the "like" charged particles, particles that came from the cloth: namely, electrons. Assist students in following the Procedure given on STUDENT HANDOUT—LESSON 24. Give them time to make their observations and answer the questions as directed.

Observations & Analysis

- Students should draw the balloons moving apart as they have become coated with "like" charged particles.
- *Answer to the question:* Students should observe that the "like" electrical charges on the balloons (i.e., the electrons) cause them to repel one another.

BEFORE RUBBING THE BALLOONS WITH WOOL OR SILK CLOTH

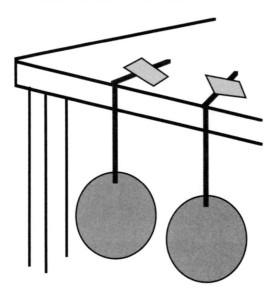

AFTER RUBBING THE BALLOONS WITH WOOL OR SILK CLOTH

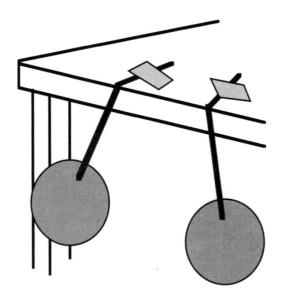

Physical Science

STUDENT HANDOUT–LESSON 24

Basic Principle   Electricity and magnetism are related effects that have many useful applications in daily life.

Objective   Show that electrically charged objects repel each other.

Materials   string, tape, two balloons, wool or silk cloth

Procedure   READ EACH STEP ONE SENTENCE AT A TIME.

1. Inflate two balloons to equal size and tie them closed.

2. Cut two equal lengths of string. Tie the string to the ends of the balloons.

3. Tape the free ends of string to the edge of a table. Allow the balloons to hang over the edge several inches apart.

4. Rub the balloons with wool or silk cloth.

5. Observe what happens and record your observations.

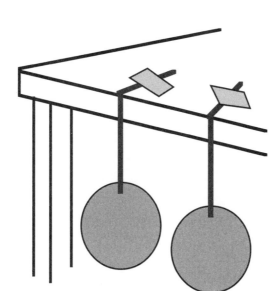

Observations & Analysis

1. Draw what happened after you rubbed the two balloons with wool or silk cloth.

2. Explain your observations.

_____

_____

_____

_____

_____

_____

_____

Lesson 25: Teacher Preparation

Basic Principle   Electricity and magnetism are related effects that have many useful applications in daily life.

Competency   Students will show that magnets have two poles.

Materials   compass, bowl, water, sponge, bar magnets

Procedure   Draw Illustration A to remind students that the Earth is surrounded by a magnetic field. A natural or manmade magnet that is free to move will align itself with that field. For this reason we call the pole on the magnet that points north the *north pole of the magnet*. We call the pole that points south the *south pole of the magnet*. Assist students in following the Procedure given on STUDENT HANDOUT—LESSON 25. Give them time to make their observations and answer the questions as directed.

Observations & Analysis

- Students should record the fact that the bar magnet floating on the sponge points in the same direction as the compass needle.
- *Answer to the question:* Students should mention that we name the poles of a magnet after the north and south directions on a map.

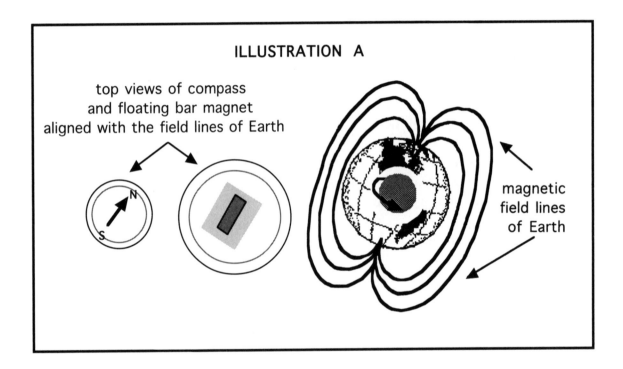

Physical Science
STUDENT HANDOUT–LESSON 25

Basic Principle Electricity and magnetism are related effects that have many useful applications in daily life.

Objective Show that magnets have two poles.

Materials compass, bowl, water, sponge, bar magnet

Procedure READ EACH STEP ONE SENTENCE AT A TIME.

1. Fill a bowl with water.

2. Float a dry sponge in the water.

3. Place a bar magnet on the sponge and allow it to float freely.

4. Place a compass next to the bowl.

5. Compare the direction of the bar magnet with the direction of the compass needle.

Observations & Analysis

1. Record your observations.

_____

_____

_____

_____

2. Why do you think we call the different ends of a magnet the "north pole" and the "south pole"?

_____

_____

_____

_____

_____

_____

_____

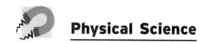

Lesson 26: Teacher Preparation

Basic Principle   Electricity and magnetism are related effects that have many useful applications in daily life.

Competency   Students will show that the like poles of magnets repel one another while unlike poles attract.

Materials   string, bar magnets, tape

Procedure   Assist students in following the Procedure given on STUDENT HANDOUT—LESSON 26. Give them time to make their observations and answer the questions as directed. Summarize the activity by having students write the following law of magnetics: *The like poles of magnets repel while the unlike poles attract.*

Observations & Analysis

- *Answer to question 1:* Students should record that the two north poles repelled one another.

- *Answer to question 2:* Students should record that the two south poles repelled one another.

- *Answer to question 3:* Students should record that the north pole attracted the south pole.

- *Answer to question 4:* The like poles of magnets repel while the unlike poles attract.

REPELLING LIKE MAGNETIC POLES

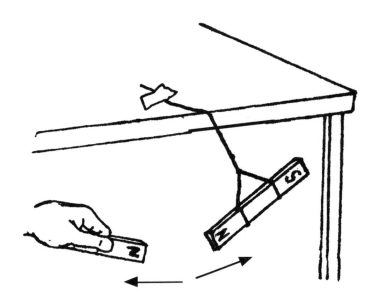

ATTRACTING UNLIKE MAGNETIC POLES

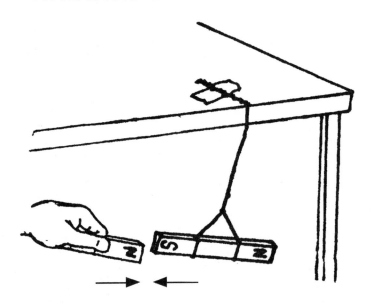

Name _____ **Date** _____

Physical Science
STUDENT HANDOUT–LESSON 26

Basic Principle   Electricity and magnetism are related effects that have many useful applications in daily life.

Objective   Show that the like poles of magnets repel one another while unlike poles attract.

Materials   string, bar magnets, tape

Procedure   READ EACH STEP ONE SENTENCE AT A TIME.

1. Tie a string around a bar magnet as shown.

2. Hang the magnet over the edge of a table. Tape the string in place and allow the magnet to swing freely until it comes to rest.

3. Bring another bar magnet close to the hanging magnet.

4. Observe what happens when you place "like poles," such as north-to-north or south-to-south, close together. Record your observations.

5. Observe what happens when you place the "unlike poles," north-to-south, close together. Record your observations.

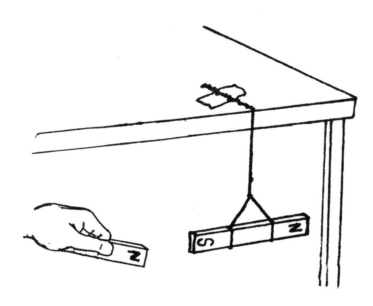

Observations & Analysis

1. Explain what you observed when you placed the north pole of one magnet near the north pole of the other magnet.

   _____

   _____

   _____

   _____

2. Explain what you observed when you placed the south pole of one magnet near the south pole of the other magnet.

   _____

   _____

   _____

   _____

3. Explain what you observed when you placed the north pole of one magnet near the south pole of the other magnet.

   _____

   _____

   _____

   _____

4. Write a rule that describes the behavior of magnets.

   _____

   _____

   _____

   _____

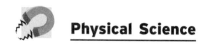

Lesson 27: Teacher Preparation

Basic Principle   Electricity and magnetism are related effects that have many useful applications in daily life.

Competency   Students will draw the magnetic field lines around a bar magnet to illustrate the force field surrounding it.

Materials   paper towels, looseleaf paper, bar magnets, iron filings

Procedure   Assist students in following the Procedure given on STUDENT HANDOUT—LESSON 27. Give them time to make their observations and complete the drawings as directed.

Observations & Analysis   Refer to the drawings shown here.

FIELD LINES SURROUNDING A BAR MAGNET

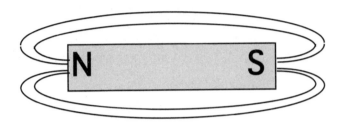

FIELD LINES SURROUNDING THE LIKE POLES OF A BAR MAGNET

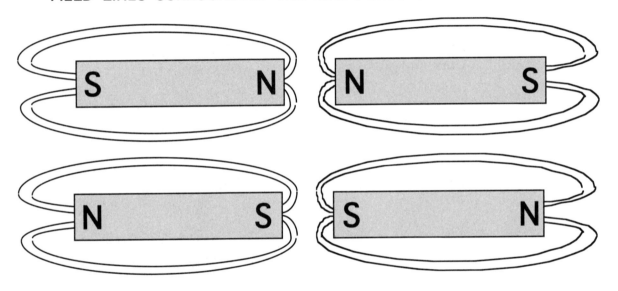

FIELD LINES SURROUNDING UNLIKE POLES OF A BAR MAGNET

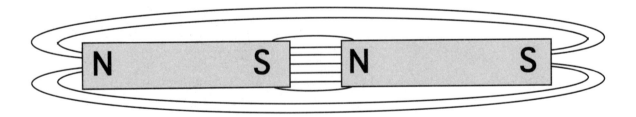

Name _____ **Date** _____

Physical Science
STUDENT HANDOUT–LESSON 27

Basic Principle   Electricity and magnetism are related effects that have many useful applications in daily life.

Objective   Draw the magnetic field lines around a bar magnet to illustrate the force fields surrounding it.

Materials   paper towels, looseleaf paper, two bar magnets, iron filings

Procedure   READ EACH STEP ONE SENTENCE AT A TIME.

1. Place a bar magnet on a paper towel.

2. Place a clean white piece of looseleaf paper on top of the bar magnet.

3. Sprinkle iron filings on the looseleaf paper over the magnet. BE SURE TO COVER THE LENGTH OF THE MAGNET.

4. Draw your observations in the *Observations & Analysis* section.

5. Remove the looseleaf paper and place the unlike poles of two bar magnets an inch apart on the paper towel.

6. Put the looseleaf paper on top of both magnets. Spread the iron filings over the length of both magnets using your fingers. Draw your observations in the *Observations & Analysis* section.

7. Remove the looseleaf paper and place the like poles of two bar magnets an inch apart on the paper towel.

8. Put the looseleaf paper on top of both magnets. Spread the iron filings over the length of both magnets using your fingers. Draw your observations in the *Observations & Analysis* section.

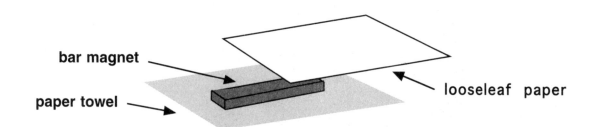

bar magnet

paper towel

looseleaf paper

Observations & Analysis

1. Draw the arrangement of iron filings on the looseleaf paper over a single bar magnet.

2. Draw the arrangement of iron filings on the looseleaf paper over two bar magnets with facing north poles.

3. Draw the arrangement of iron filings on the looseleaf paper over two bar magnets with facing south poles.

4. Draw the arrangement of iron filings on the looseleaf paper over two bar magnets with facing unlike poles.

Lesson 28: Teacher Preparation

Basic Principle   Electricity and magnetism are related effects that have many useful applications in daily life.

Competency   Students will demonstrate that electrical energy is quickly changed to heat energy.

Materials   battery, tape, switch, thin-gauge insulated copper wire, alligator clips, beaker, water, thermometer

Procedure   Prepare for the lesson by stripping the insulation off the ends of 4-inch to 6-inch lengths of thin-gauge insulated copper wire as done in previous lessons. Connect alligator clips to the bare ends of each section of wire. Make sure all switches are in the "open" position. Place D-cell batteries in battery holders that facilitate clip connections. Assist students in constructing the circuits shown here and on STUDENT HANDOUT—LESSON 28. **WARN STUDENTS NOT TO TOUCH THE WATER WHILE THE SWITCH IS CLOSED.** Give them time to read, record, and plot their results on the graph provided. Monitor students to make sure none of the wires begin to overheat.

Observations & Analysis   *Answer to the question:* Students will record a rise in water temperature as the wire begins to heat. Explain that even the best electrical conductors (e.g., copper) have some resistance to the flow of electric current. This resistance is caused by the friction between the stationary atoms in the wire and the passing electrical current.

WARNING!

DO NOT TOUCH THE WATER IN THE BEAKER WHILE THE SWITCH IS CLOSED AND THE CURRENT IS FLOWING.

IMMEDIATELY OPEN THE SWITCH TO TURN OFF THE CURRENT IF THE WIRE BEGINS TO OVERHEAT.

OPEN THE SWITCH AND STOP THE DEMONSTRATION AFTER THREE MINUTES.

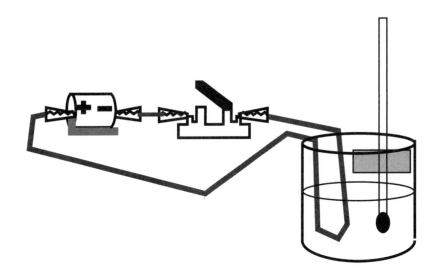

Name _____ **Date** _____

Physical Science

STUDENT HANDOUT–LESSON 28

Basic Principle   Electricity and magnetism are related effects that have many useful applications in daily life.

Objective   Demonstrate that electrical energy is quickly changed to heat energy.

Materials   battery, tape, switch, thin-gauge insulated wire, beaker, water, thermometer

Procedure   READ EACH STEP ONE SENTENCE AT A TIME.

1. Tape a thermometer to the inside of a small beaker.

2. Fill the beaker about halfway with water.

3. Build the circuit shown. Bend and insert a section of insulated wire into the water. **MAKE SURE THE SWITCH IS OPEN.**

4. Record the temperature of the water on the graph in the _Observations & Analysis_ section.

5. Close the switch and record the temperature of the water every twenty seconds for three minutes. **OPEN THE SWITCH IMMEDIATELY IF ANY SMOKE APPEARS ANYWHERE IN THE CIRCUIT.**

6. Open the switch at the end of three minutes.

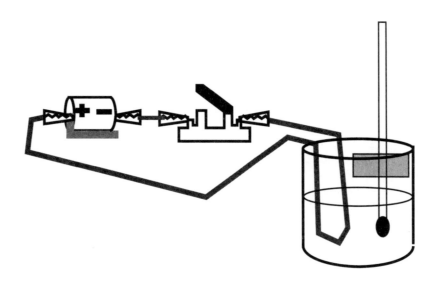

Observations & Analysis

1. Close the switch and record the temperature of the water every twenty seconds for three minutes. **OPEN THE SWITCH IMMEDIATELY IF ANY SMOKE APPEARS ANYWHERE IN THE CIRCUIT.** Open the switch at the end of three minutes.

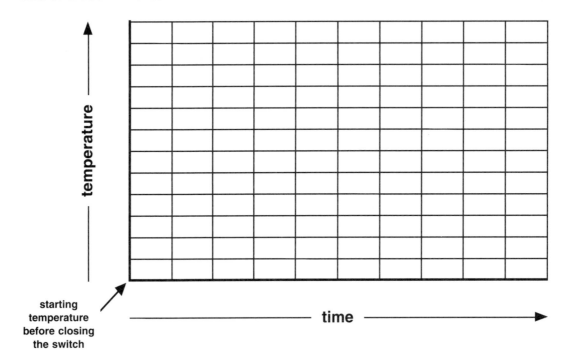

starting
temperature
before closing
the switch

2. Summarize your graph and explain your results.

_____

_____

_____

_____

_____

_____

_____

_____

_____

_____

_____

_____

Lesson 29: Teacher Preparation

Basic Principle   Electricity and magnetism are related effects that have many useful applications in daily life.

Competency   Students will build a lightbulb to show how electrical energy is changed to light energy.

Materials   small glass jar, fine thread of iron picture-hanging wire, pencil, thin-gauge insulated wire, battery, switch, alligator clips, modeling clay

Procedure   Prepare for the lesson by uncoiling strands of iron picture-hanging wire to separate the thin metal threads. Students will use a thin metal thread of the wire as the filament for the lightbulb constructed in this lesson. Strip the insulation off the ends of 4-inch to 6-inch lengths of thin-gauge insulated copper wire as done in previous lessons. Connect alligator clips to the bare ends of each section of wire. MAKE SURE ALL SWITCHES ARE IN THE "OPEN" POSITION. Place D-cell batteries in battery holders that facilitate clip connections. Assist students in constructing the lightbulb and circuits shown here and on STUDENT HANDOUT—LESSON 29. Give them time to answer the questions as directed.

Observations & Analysis

- *Answer to question 1:* The thin metal thread of the wire serving as the filament for the lightbulb began to glow.

- *Answer to question 2:* The heat produced as the result of friction between the fixed atoms in the wire and the passing electrical current caused the filament to get "red hot."

- *Answer to question 3:* Answers will vary but can include any number of logical reasons, including one or both of the following explanations: (A) The connections were loose. (B) The battery was not strong enough to overcome the resistance in the wires of the circuit.

COMPLETED LIGHTBULB

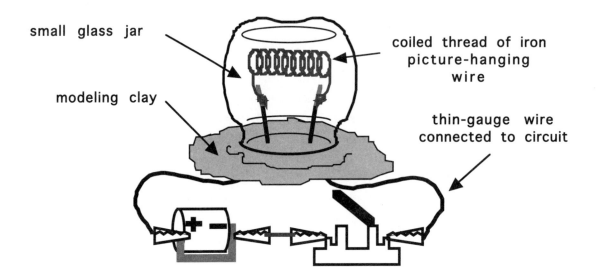

small glass jar

coiled thread of iron picture-hanging wire

modeling clay

thin-gauge wire connected to circuit

Physical Science
STUDENT HANDOUT–LESSON 29

Basic Principle   Electricity and magnetism are related effects that have many useful applications in daily life.

Objective   Build a lightbulb to show how electrical energy is changed to light energy.

Materials   small glass jar, fine thread of iron picture-hanging wire, pencil, thin-gauge insulated wire, battery, switch, modeling clay

Procedure   READ EACH STEP ONE SENTENCE AT A TIME.

1. Coil a three-inch thread of iron picture-hanging wire around a pencil and then remove the pencil.

2. Flatten a piece of modeling clay large enough to fit over the mouth of a small glass jar.

3. Build the circuit shown here and stick the two stripped ends of thin-gauge insulated wire through the clay. **MAKE SURE THE SWITCH IS OPEN AND THE BARE ENDS OF THE WIRE DO NOT TOUCH.**

4. Tightly wind the ends of the coil of iron picture-hanging wire to the bare ends of thin-gauge wire sticking out of the clay.

5. Put the mouth of the jar over the coil and press it into the clay base. Your lightbulb should look like the picture shown.

6. Close the switch. If the iron picture-hanging wire does not begin to glow within fifteen seconds, then open the switch and check your connections. Let the iron picture-hanging wire glow for ten seconds before you open the switch and stop the flow of electric current.

COMPLETED LIGHTBULB

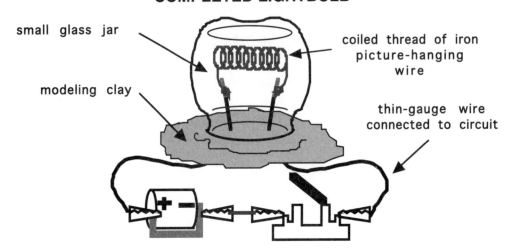

small glass jar

coiled thread of iron picture-hanging wire

modeling clay

thin-gauge wire connected to circuit

Observations & Analysis

1. What happened when you closed the switch?

_____

_____

_____

2. Explain why the coil glows.

_____

_____

_____

_____

_____

3. Explain what might have gone wrong if the coil did not glow.

_____

_____

_____

_____

_____

Lesson 30: Teacher Preparation

Basic Principle   Electricity and magnetism are related effects that have many useful applications in daily life.

Competency   Students will build a battery to show how chemical energy is changed to electrical energy.

Materials   aluminum foil, paper towel, flashlight bulb, battery, thin-gauge insulated wire, switch, small pieces of insulated copper lamp wire, plastic cups, bleach

Procedure

1. Prepare for the lesson by stripping the insulation off the ends of 4-inch to 6-inch lengths of thin-gauge insulated copper wire as done in previous lessons. Connect alligator clips to the bare ends of each section of wire. Insert appropriate flashlight bulbs into their sockets. MAKE SURE ALL SWITCHES ARE IN THE "OPEN" POSITION. Place D-cell batteries in battery holders that facilitate clip connections. Cut small lengths of insulated copper lamp wire and strip the ends off the wire. Twist and bundle the threads of copper wire inside the insulation to form a "wire-ball" at one end of half of the sections. One plain section of lamp wire and one section with a wireball will be needed to construct each battery.

2. The Italian scientist Count Alesandro Volta (1745–1827) invented the first battery in 1800. His invention was called a *voltaic pile*. A battery is a chemical tool for separating stores of positive (+) and negative (–) electric charges (i.e., protons and electrons, respectively).

3. Assist students in constructing the circuits and battery as instructed in the Procedure on STUDENT HANDOUT—LESSON 30. **WARN STUDENTS TO KEEP CLEAR OF THE BLEACH AS YOU ADD THE SOLUTION TO EACH CUP.** Explain that bleach is a solution that contains an *electrolyte*. Define an *electrolyte* as any substance that will conduct electricity when mixed with water. Salt is another example of an electrolyte. Give students time to make their observation and answer questions as directed.

Observations & Analysis

- *Answer to question 1:* The lightbulb began to glow.
- *Answer to question 2:* The chemical bleach reacted with the metal in the aluminum foil to produce electricity. The heat produced as the result of friction between the fixed atoms in the wire and the passing electrical current caused the filament to get "red hot."
- *Answer to question 3:* Answers will vary but can include any number of logical reasons, including one or both of the following explanations: (A) The connections were loose. (B) The chemical reaction was not strong enough to produce enough electricity to overcome the resistance in the wires of the circuit.

WARNING!

DO NOT INHALE THE FUMES
FROM THE BLEACH IN THE CUP.

DO NOT TOUCH THE BLEACH
OR SPILL IT ON CLOTHING.

CHEMICAL BATTERY

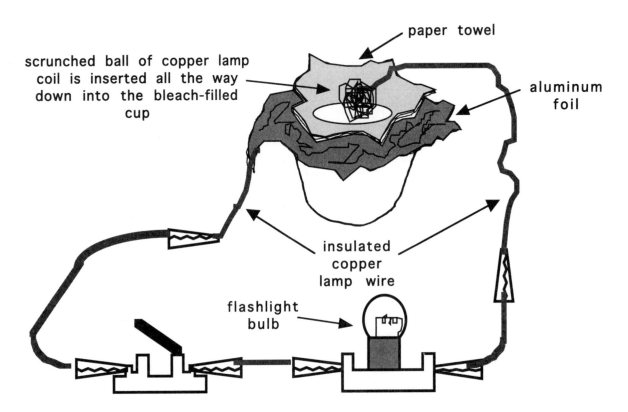

paper towel

scrunched ball of copper lamp coil is inserted all the way down into the bleach-filled cup

aluminum foil

insulated copper lamp wire

flashlight bulb

Name _____ **Date** _____

Physical Science
STUDENT HANDOUT–LESSON 30

Basic Principle   Electricity and magnetism are related effects that have many useful applications in daily life.

Objective   Build a battery to show how chemical energy is changed to electrical energy.

Materials   aluminum foil, paper towel, flashlight bulb, battery, thin-gauge insulated wire, switch, two small pieces of insulated copper lamp wire, plastic cup, bleach

Procedure   READ EACH STEP ONE SENTENCE AT A TIME.

1. Connect the battery, switch, flashlight bulb, thin-gauge insulated wire, and sections of lamp cord to build the circuit shown here.

2. Completely line the inside of the plastic cup with a single piece of aluminum foil. Twist and drape a section of aluminum foil over the edge of the cup.

3. Line the aluminum foil with the paper towel. MAKE SURE NONE OF THE PAPER TOWEL DRAPE OVER THE EDGE OF THE CUP.

4. Put the "scrunched ball" of copper lamp coil all the way down into the cup.

5. Connect the other section of copper lamp coil to the aluminum foil hanging over the edge of the cup.

6. Sit back away from the cup. Allow your teacher to pour the bleach into the cup. **DO NOT INHALE THE FUMES FROM THE BLEACH.**

7. Close the switch as soon as the cup is filled with bleach and record your observations.

8. Open the switch after the flashlight bulb glows for ten seconds.

CHEMICAL BATTERY

scrunched ball of copper lamp
coil is inserted all the way
down into the bleach-filled
cup

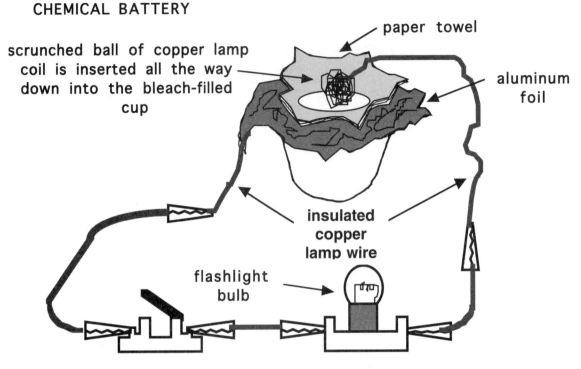

paper towel

aluminum
foil

insulated
copper
lamp wire

flashlight
bulb

Observations & Analysis

1. What happened when you closed the switch?

_____

_____

_____

2. Explain your observations.

_____

_____

_____

_____

3. Explain what might have gone wrong if the bulb did not light.

_____

_____

_____

_____

FOURTH-GRADE LEVEL

Physical Science

PRACTICE TEST

Physical Science

PRACTICE TEST

Directions: Use the diagrams of the electric circuits shown below to answer questions 1 through 7. (Use the Answer Sheet.)

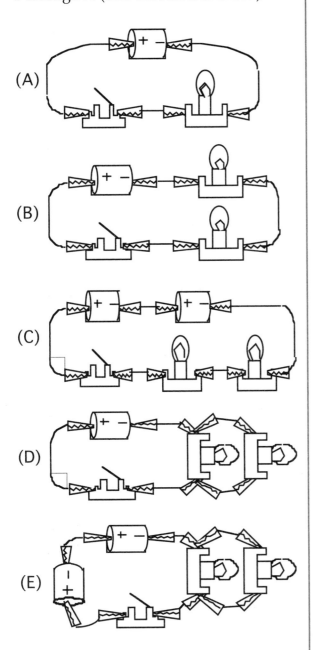

(A)

(B)

(C)

(D)

(E)

1. Which diagram(s) show a series circuit? You may darken more than one letter on your Answer Sheet.

2. Which diagram(s) show a parallel circuit? You may darken more than one letter on your Answer Sheet.

3. Which series circuit would have the dimmest bulbs when the switch is closed?

4. Which parallel circuit would have the brightest bulbs when the switch is closed?

5. What would happen if one bulb in circuit "B" blew out after closing the switch?

   (A) The good bulb would still glow with the same brightness.

   (B) The good bulb would get brighter.

   (C) The good bulb would get dimmer.

   (D) The good bulb would go out.

   (E) The good bulb would start flashing on and off.

6. What would happen if one bulb in circuit "D" blew out after closing the switch?

   (A) The good bulb would glow with the same brightness.

   (B) The good bulb would get brighter.

   (C) The good bulb would get dimmer.

   (D) The good bulb would go out.

   (E) The good bulb would start flashing on and off.

7. Which of the following would be true after the switch is closed?

   (A) Circuit A's bulbs are brighter than C's bulbs.

   (B) Circuit B's bulbs are dimmer than D's bulbs.

   (C) Circuit A's bulbs are brighter than D's bulbs.

   (D) Circuit C's bulbs are brighter than E's bulbs.

   (E) All the bulbs would be the same brightness.

Directions: Use the Answer Sheet to darken the letter of the choice that best answers each question.

8. Which of the following is most like the Earth's rotating core?

   (A) a battery

   (B) a magnet

   (C) a motor

   (D) an engine

   (E) a piece of lead

9. What would normally happen to a bar magnet hung from a length of string as shown?

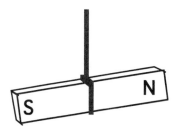

   (A) It would point north.

   (B) It would point east.

   (C) It would point west.

   (D) It would point toward the sky.

   (E) It would point toward the ground.

10. Where does a compass normally point?

   (A) north

   (B) east

   (C) west

   (D) up

   (E) down

11. What is the best way to turn an iron nail into a magnet?

    (A) Attach the nail to a battery.

    (B) Stroke the nail repeatedly in one direction with a magnet.

    (C) Stroke the nail repeatedly back and forth with a magnet.

    (D) Use a furnace to melt the nail together with a magnet, then allow the molten metal to cool.

    (E) An iron nail cannot be magnetized.

12. What would normally happen to the compass needle shown below when the circuit switch is closed?

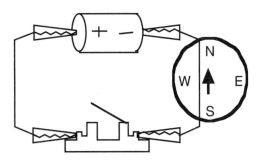

    (A) It would continue to point north.

    (B) It would reverse direction and point south.

    (C) It would point toward the switch.

    (D) It would point toward the battery.

    (E) It would point to the right.

13. Which of the following lists the necessary materials needed to make an electromagnet?

    (A) insulated wire and iron nail

    (B) battery and insulated wire

    (C) battery, paper clips, iron nail

    (D) insulated wire, tape, paper clips, iron filings

    (E) battery, insulated wire, iron nail

14. Which of the following makes it possible to build a motor?

    (A) All compasses point north.

    (B) Magnets are made of iron.

    (C) Magnets are inexpensive.

    (D) Electromagnets do not need batteries.

    (E) An electric current creates a magnetic field.

15. Which of the following tools is used to detect electric charges?

    (A) a battery

    (B) a motor

    (C) a telescope

    (D) an electroscope

    (E) a microscope

16. How would the two balloons shown below behave after being rubbed with wool?

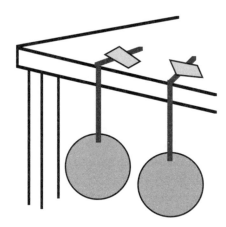

(A) They would continue to hang straight down.

(B) They would attract one another.

(C) They would repel one another.

(D) They would expand.

(E) They would be attracted to the wooden parts of the table.

Directions: Use the Answer Sheet to darken the letter that best completes sentences 17 through 22.

17. The north poles of two bar magnets placed very close together would _____.

(A) strongly attract

(B) weakly attract

(C) strongly repel

(D) weakly repel

(E) not affect one another

18. The north poles of two bar magnets placed far apart would _____.

(A) strongly attract

(B) weakly attract

(C) strongly repel

(D) weakly repel

(E) not affect one another

19. The south poles of two bar magnets placed very close together would _____.

(A) strongly attract

(B) weakly attract

(C) strongly repel

(D) weakly repel

(E) not affect one another

20. The south poles of two bar magnets placed far apart would _____.

(A) strongly attract

(B) weakly attract

(C) strongly repel

(D) weakly repel

(E) not affect one another

21. The north pole and south pole of two bar magnets placed very close together would _____.

(A) strongly attract

(B) weakly attract

(C) strongly repel

(D) weakly repel

(E) not affect one another

22. The north pole and south pole of two bar magnets placed far apart would _____.

    (A) strongly attract
    (B) weakly attract
    (C) strongly repel
    (D) weakly repel
    (E) not affect one another

Directions: A piece of looseleaf paper is placed over two bar magnets as shown. Then iron filings are poured onto the paper.

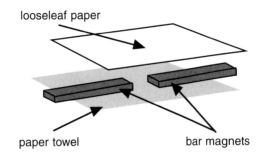

looseleaf paper

paper towel   bar magnets

Use the diagrams below to answer questions 23 through 25. (Use the Answer Sheet.)

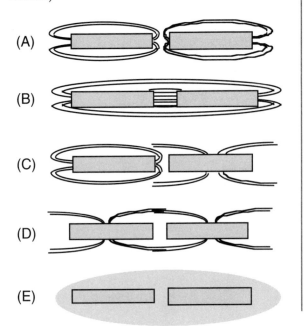

(A)

(B)

(C)

(D)

(E)

23. Which diagram best describes the arrangement of iron filings on the paper when two north poles are placed close together?

24. Which diagram best describes the arrangement of iron filings on the paper when two south poles are placed close together?

25. Which diagram best describes the arrangement of iron filings on the paper when a north pole and a south pole are placed close together?

Physical Science

PRACTICE TEST: ANSWER SHEET

Name _____ **Date** _____ **Period** _____

Darken the circle above the letter that best answers the question.

1. ○ A ○ B ○ C ○ D ○ E   14. ○ A ○ B ○ C ○ D ○ E

2. ○ A ○ B ○ C ○ D ○ E   15. ○ A ○ B ○ C ○ D ○ E

3. ○ A ○ B ○ C ○ D ○ E   16. ○ A ○ B ○ C ○ D ○ E

4. ○ A ○ B ○ C ○ D ○ E   17. ○ A ○ B ○ C ○ D ○ E

5. ○ A ○ B ○ C ○ D ○ E   18. ○ A ○ B ○ C ○ D ○ E

6. ○ A ○ B ○ C ○ D ○ E   19. ○ A ○ B ○ C ○ D ○ E

7. ○ A ○ B ○ C ○ D ○ E   20. ○ A ○ B ○ C ○ D ○ E

8. ○ A ○ B ○ C ○ D ○ E   21. ○ A ○ B ○ C ○ D ○ E

9. ○ A ○ B ○ C ○ D ○ E   22. ○ A ○ B ○ C ○ D ○ E

10. ○ A ○ B ○ C ○ D ○ E   23. ○ A ○ B ○ C ○ D ○ E

11. ○ A ○ B ○ C ○ D ○ E   24. ○ A ○ B ○ C ○ D ○ E

12. ○ A ○ B ○ C ○ D ○ E   25. ○ A ○ B ○ C ○ D ○ E

13. ○ A ○ B ○ C ○ D ○ E

Physical Science

KEY TO PRACTICE TEST

1. ● A ● B ● C ○ D ○ E
2. ○ A ○ B ○ C ● D ● E
3. ○ A ● B ○ C ○ D ○ E
4. ○ A ○ B ○ C ○ D ● E
5. ○ A ○ B ○ C ● D ○ E
6. ● A ○ B ○ C ○ D ○ E
7. ○ A ● B ○ C ○ D ○ E
8. ○ A ● B ○ C ○ D ○ E
9. ● A ○ B ○ C ○ D ○ E
10. ● A ○ B ○ C ○ D ○ E
11. ○ A ● B ○ C ○ D ○ E
12. ○ A ○ B ○ C ○ D ● E
13. ○ A ○ B ○ C ○ D ● E

14. ○ A ○ B ○ C ○ D ● E
15. ○ A ○ B ○ C ● D ○ E
16. ○ A ○ B ● C ○ D ○ E
17. ○ A ○ B ● C ○ D ○ E
18. ○ A ○ B ○ C ● D ○ E
19. ○ A ○ B ● C ○ D ○ E
20. ○ A ○ B ○ C ● D ○ E
21. ● A ○ B ○ C ○ D ○ E
22. ○ A ● B ○ C ○ D ○ E
23. ● A ○ B ○ C ○ D ○ E
24. ● A ○ B ○ C ○ D ○ E
25. ○ A ● B ○ C ○ D ○ E

Section III: Life Science

LESSONS AND ACTIVITIES

Lesson 31 Students will show that plants are attracted to sunlight to obtain their energy.

Lesson 32 Students will show that plants deprived of sunlight cannot survive.

Lesson 33 Students will observe that plants make starch in the presence of sunlight.

Lesson 34 Students will identify foods that have starch, a primary food source for animals in the food chain.

Lesson 35 Students will classify organisms as either producers or consumers of food.

Lesson 36 Students will classify animals as herbivores, carnivores, or omnivores.

Lesson 37 Students will construct a "food chain" to show that plants, herbivores, carnivores, and omnivores depend on one another for survival.

Lesson 38 Students will draw a chart of a "food pyramid" to show how primary and secondary consumers compete for resources in an ecosystem.

Lesson 39 Students will show that microorganisms cause decomposition.

Lesson 40 Students will discuss the eating habits of insects to explain how they help recycle matter from dead plants and animals to living organisms.

Lesson 41 Students will list the living and nonliving resources in different ecosystems.

Lesson 42 Students will discuss how the survival of living organisms depends on nonliving resources in the environment.

Lesson 43 Students will show that for any particular environment some kinds of organisms survive well, some survive less well, and some cannot survive at all.

Lesson 44 Students will show that many microorganisms do not cause disease and can be beneficial to other living organisms.

Lesson 45 Students will show that many plants depend on insects and animals for pollination and seed dispersal.

LIFE SCIENCE PRACTICE TEST

Lesson 31: Teacher Preparation

Basic Principle   All organisms need energy and matter to live and grow.

Competency   Students will show that plants are attracted to sunlight to obtain their energy.

Materials   small house plants, paper or Styrofoam cups, potting soil, sunlight, water

Procedure   Prepare for the lesson by potting small plants in individual paper or Styrofoam cups. Make sure all plants are adequately watered during the course of the experiment.

Observations & Analysis   *Answer to the question:* A plant seeks out sunlight by turning its leaves toward the light. This kind of movement by plants is called *phototropism*. The prefix "photo-" means *light*. "Tropism" means *movement*.

DAY 1: A potted plant is placed by a sunny window with its leaves turned away from the sunlight.

DAYS 2 and 3: The leaves of the plant will move progressively toward the sunlight until the topside of the leaves are facing the sun.

Life Science
STUDENT HANDOUT–LESSON 31

Basic Principle   All organisms need energy and matter to live and grow.

Objective   Show that plants are attracted to sunlight.

Materials   small house plant, paper or Styrofoam cup, potting soil, sunlight, water

Procedure

1. Pour some potting soil into a paper or Styrofoam cup.

2. Moisten the soil with several teaspoons of water.

3. Use your finger to poke a hole in the soil and insert the roots and stem of the small house plant given to you by your teacher.

4. Place your plant on a windowsill facing the sun. Make sure the leaves are pointing away from the window.

5. Draw the position of the plant's leaves in the box marked "DAY 1." Write a brief description of the position of the leaves.

6. Wait two days.

7. Draw the position of the leaves in the box marked "DAY 2." Write a brief description of the position of the leaves. Turn the plant so that the leaves face away from the window. Add one teaspoon of water to the soil.

8. Wait two days.

9. Draw the position of the leaves in the box marked "DAY 3." Write a brief description of the position of the leaves.

10. Use your drawings to explain your observations.

Observations & Analysis   Summarize your observations in one or two sentences using your drawings.

_____

_____

_____

Why do you think the leaves behaved the way they did?

_____

_____

_____

_____

DAY 1	Observations on Day 1:

DAY 2	Observations on Day 2:

DAY 3	Observations on Day 3:

Lesson 32: Teacher Preparation

Basic Principle   All organisms need energy and matter to live and grow.

Competency   Students will show that plants deprived of sunlight cannot survive.

Materials   small house plants, paper or Styrofoam cups, potting soil, sunlight, water, dark construction paper, scissors, tape

Procedure   Prepare small house plants for potting in individual paper or Styrofoam cups. Make sure all plants are adequately watered during the course of the experiment.

Observations & Analysis   *Answer to the question:* The leaves that were deprived of sunlight withered and died. Students should observe that the "starved" leaves lost their green color. Healthy leaves contain an "energy-trapping" chemical called *chlorophyll*. The prefix "chloro-" means *color*. The term "-phyll" means *to love*. In the absence of sunlight, chlorophyll is broken down by the chemical actions of the plant, which does not have sufficient energy to replace the lost supply. The leaf dies without chlorophyll to trap the energy of the sun.

LEAVES DEPRIVED OF SUNLIGHT WILL WITHER AND DIE.
THE CHLOROPHYLL IN THE COVERED LEAVES WILL BE
BROKEN DOWN BY THE CHEMICAL ACTION OF THE PLANT
WITHOUT ENERGY TO REPLENISH THE SUPPLY.

Name _____ **Date** _____

Life Science

STUDENT HANDOUT–LESSON 32

Basic Principle All organisms need energy and matter to live and grow.

Objective Show that plants deprived of sunlight cannot survive.

Materials small house plants, paper or Styrofoam cups, potting soil, sunlight, water, dark construction paper, scissors, tape

Procedure

1. Pour some potting soil into a paper or Styrofoam cup.

2. Moisten the soil with several teaspoons of water.

3. Use your finger to poke a hole in the soil and insert the roots and stem of the small house plant given to you by your teacher.

4. Refer to Figure A. Cut out two pieces of dark construction paper about twice the size of the leaves on the plant.

5. Fold each piece of paper around a leaf. Use tape to close the paper around each leaf. Be sure no part of these leaves is exposed to sunlight.

6. Place your plant on a windowsill facing the sun.

7. Wait one week.

8. Remove the tape carefully and uncover the two leaves.

9. Draw your observations in the box.

Observations & Analysis   Compare the texture of each leaf to the leaves that were not covered with construction paper. What happened to the texture of each leaf?

_____

_____

_____

Compare the color of each leaf to the leaves that were not covered with construction paper. What happened to the color of each leaf?

_____

_____

_____

_____

Explain your observations.

_____

_____

_____

FIGURE A	DRAWING OF PLANT LEAVES AFTER A WEEK
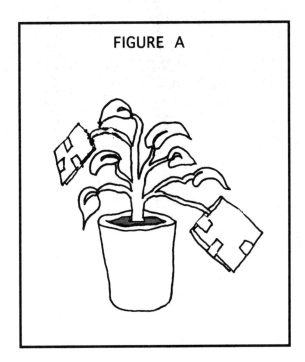	

Life Science

Lesson 33: Teacher Preparation

Basic Principle   All organisms need energy and matter to live and grow.

Competency   Students will observe that plants make starch in the presence of sunlight.

Materials   two hot plates, 250-mL beaker, two 1,000-mL beakers, 500-mL beaker, water, tongs, Lugol's solution (see below), healthy green leafy plant, aluminum foil, tape, sunlight, ethyl alcohol, medicine dropper, paper towels, safetywear (i.e., heat-resistant gloves, goggles)

Procedure

1. Prepare for this lesson by taping aluminum foil over the top and bottom of one-half of a dozen leaves of a healthy green plant (geranium leaves work great). Place the plant in sunlight (e.g., 12 hours light, then 12 hours dark) for 24–48 hours.

2. Students will watch you demonstrate that plants produce starch in the presence of sunlight. Students will record the procedure used in the demonstration.

3. **SAFETY PRECAUTIONS: BOILING WATER AND ALCOHOL CAN CAUSE SERIOUS INJURY.** Wear goggles, heat-resistant gloves, and an apron through your demonstration. Be sure you are familiar with the proper use of the hot plate. Discard materials and clean up only after the apparatus has cooled.

4. Have students record your procedure as you perform this demonstration: (1) Carefully remove the aluminum foil from the leaves and place them in the 1,000-mL beaker of boiling water on the hot plate. Allow the leaves to boil for 5 minutes to help soften them (i.e., break down cell walls). (2) While you are waiting for the leaves to soften, pour 250 mL of water into another 1,000-mL beaker and place the beaker on a second hot plate on medium-high setting. (3) Pour 300 mL of ethyl alcohol into a 500-mL beaker and place it in the water in the 1,000-mL beaker on the second hot plate. (4) Use tongs to transfer the boiled leaves into the beaker of alcohol and wait 5–10 minutes for the leaves to lose their green color. (5) Use tongs to remove the wet leaves from the alcohol and turn off the hot plates. (6) Rinse the leaves with cool water and place them on paper towels. (7) Soak the leaves in a 250-mL beaker of Lugol's solution for 3–5 minutes. NOTE: Lugol's solution tests for the presence of starch and can be purchased from any laboratory supply house. You can prepare your own Lugol's solution by dissolving 10 grams of potassium iodide in 100 mL of distilled water and adding 5 grams of iodine crystals to the solution. (8) Remove and rinse the leaves again in cool water. (9) Distribute the leaves for examination by the students.

Observations & Analysis

- *Answer to question 1:* The teacher wore goggles and gloves to protect his/her eyes and hands from injury while using hot water and alcohol.

- *Answer to question 3:* The covered side of the leaf does not display the blackish presence of starch. Plants only produce starch in the presence of sunlight.

DEMONSTRATION

1,000-mL beaker
with boiled water
on hot plate

500-mL beaker with 300 mL ethyl alcohol
placed in 1,000-mL beaker with 250 mL
warm water on hot plate

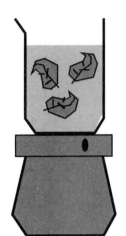

FIRST HOT PLATE

SECOND HOT PLATE

beaker of Lugol's solution

Life Science

STUDENT HANDOUT–LESSON 33

Basic Principle   All organisms need energy and matter to live and grow.

Objective   Observe that plants make starch in the presence of sunlight.

Materials   paper and colored pencils

Procedure   Watch carefully as your teacher performs this demonstration. Write a brief sentence to describe each step of the experiment.

1. _____
   _____

2. _____
   _____

3. _____
   _____

4. _____
   _____

5. _____
   _____

6. _____
   _____

7. _____
   _____

8. _____
   _____

Observations & Analysis

1. Why did the teacher wear goggles and heat-resistant gloves?

_____

_____

_____

_____

_____

2. Draw and color the leaf your teacher gave you. Show the positions of each dark starch stain.

3. Why are most of the stains found on only one-half of the leaf?

_____

_____

_____

_____

_____

Lesson 34: Teacher Preparation

Basic Principle   All organisms need energy and matter to live and grow.

Competency   Students will identify foods that have starch, a primary food source for animals in the food chain.

Materials   iodine, eyedropper, water, marking pen (or colored pencils or crayons), kitchen knife, teaspoon, small bowl, paper towel, beans, potatoes, bread, lettuce leaves, egg, ground beef, chicken, fish

Procedure

1. Assist students in carefully following the Procedure on STUDENT HANDOUT—LESSON 34. Make sure they exercise common-sense safety precautions when using the knife and the iodine.

2. **GIVE STUDENTS EXPLICIT WARNING THAT IODINE IS A DANGEROUS SUBSTANCE THAT CAN CAUSE SERIOUS ILLNESS IF INHALED OR INGESTED.**

Observations & Analysis

- The foods used in this lesson that contain iodine are: beans, potatoes, bread, and leaves. The eggs, ground beef, chicken, and fish are protein-rich foods that contain little starch.

- *Answer to question 2:* beans, potatoes, bread, leaves

- *Answer to question 3:* plants

WARNING!

IODINE IS A DANGEROUS SUBSTANCE THAT CAN CAUSE SERIOUS ILLNESS IF INHALED OR INGESTED.

Life Science

STUDENT HANDOUT–LESSON 34

Basic Principle   All organisms need energy and matter to live and grow.

Objective   Identify foods that have starch, a primary food source for animals in the food chain.

Materials   iodine, eyedropper, water, marking pen (or colored pencils or crayons), kitchen knife, teaspoon, small bowl, paper towel, beans, potatoes, bread, lettuce leaves, egg, ground beef, chicken, fish

Procedure

1. Use a marking pen to draw small circles, each about the size of a quarter, on a piece of paper towel. Draw as many circles as the number of sample foods given to you by your teacher. Draw two circles for the egg. You will test both the egg yolk and the egg white of the egg.

2. Use a kitchen knife to carefully prepare small chunks of each type of food. Crack open the egg and spill the yolk and egg white into the small bowl.

3. Place each chunk of food in a circle on the paper towel. Moisten each sample with a drop or two of water using the eyedropper. Use the teaspoon to drip a small amount of egg yolk in one circle and a small amount of egg white in another circle.

4. Use the eyedropper to place a drop of iodine on each sample. Iodine turns black in the presence of starch.

   WARNING: IODINE IS A DANGEROUS SUBSTANCE. DO NOT INHALE THE FUMES OR GET ANY OF THE CHEMICAL ON YOUR CLOTHES OR IN YOUR MOUTH.

5. Record your observations.

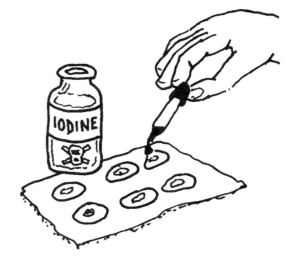

Observations & Analysis

1. Summarize your observations by drawing and coloring each food sample before and after it was treated with iodine. Label the samples that contain starch by writing the word "STARCH" under them.

2. Which foods contained the most starch? The plants? The animal meat? The egg?

_____

_____

_____

3. Which type of food is probably the primary source of energy for all living things?

_____

_____

_____

Lesson 35: Teacher Preparation

Basic Principle   Living organisms depend on one another for their survival.

Competency   Students will classify organisms as either producers or consumers of food.

Materials   magazine pictures of living organisms or the pictures shown here

Procedure

1. Remind students that the main source of energy for all living organisms on this planet is the sun. Through photosynthesis, plants trap the energy of the sun in the chlorophyll molecule, allowing the plant to store energy in the form of starch—a chemical macromolecule composed of simple sugar molecules linked in a chain. Every living thing on our planet relies on its ability to ingest foods that contain these molecules.

2. Define the terms "producer" and "consumer." Organisms that produce their own starch from sunlight, water, air, and minerals in the environment are called "producers." Plants are producers. Organisms that must eat other organisms to supply themselves with starch are called "consumers." Animals are consumers.

3. Assist students in carefully following the Procedure on STUDENT HANDOUT—LESSON 35.

Observations & Analysis

- PRODUCERS: grass, fern, sycamore, sunflower
- COMSUMERS: woodpecker, frog, newt, moth, lobster, turtle, dear, spider, fur seal, sea cow, bat, pelican, opossum, whale, sea turtle, salmon, alligator, shark
- *Answer to question 2:* Plants are producers because they make their own energy by storing the energy of the sun.
- *Answer to question 3:* Animals are consumers because they rely on plants or other animals that eat plants for their energy.

woodpecker

frog

newt

moth

lobster

turtle

grass

fern

sycamore

sunflower

spider

fur seal

sea cow

deer

pelican

opossum

salmon

whale

bat

sea turtle

shark

alligator

Name _____ **Date** _____

Life Science

STUDENT HANDOUT–LESSON 35

Basic Principle   Living organisms depend on one another for their survival.

Objective   Classify organisms as either producers or consumers of food.

Materials   pictures of living organisms

Procedure

1. Examine, identify, and name the living organisms in the pictures given to you by your teacher.

2. Discuss the eating habits of each organism with your classmates. Does the organism make its own starch from sunlight, water, air, and minerals in the environment? Or, does the organism eat other organisms that produce their own starch?

3. Organisms that produce their own starch from sunlight, water, air, and minerals in the environment are called "producers." Organisms that must eat other organisms to supply themselves with starch are called "consumers."

4. Classify each organism in the pictures given to you by your teacher as either a producer or a consumer.

5. Next to the name of each organism, list the most common foods in its diet.

Observations & Analysis

1. Classify each organism in the pictures given to you by your teacher as either a **producer** or a **consumer**. Next to the name of each organism, list the most common foods in its diet.

PRODUCERS

name   diet

_____

_____

_____

_____

_____

_____

_____

_____

_____

_____

CONSUMERS

name   diet

_____

_____

_____

_____

_____

_____

_____

_____

_____

_____

2. Which type of living organism is most likely to be a producer? Explain your answer.

_____

_____

_____

3. Which type of living organism is most likely to be a consumer? Explain your answer.

_____

_____

_____

 **Life Science**

Lesson 36: Teacher Preparation

Basic Principle   Living organisms depend on one another for their survival.

Competency   Students will classify animals as herbivores, carnivores, or omnivores.

Materials   magazine pictures of living organisms or the pictures shown here

Procedure

1. Define the terms "herbivore," "carnivore," and "omnivore." Animals that eat only or mostly plants are called "herbivores." Animals that eat only or mostly the meat of other animals, including the meat of insects, are called "carnivores." Animals that eat both plants and the meat of other animals, including the meat of insects, are called "omnivores."

2. Assist students in carefully following the Procedure on STUDENT HANDOUT—LESSON 36.

Observations & Analysis

- HERBIVORES: turtle, cow, dear

  CARNIVORES: woodpecker, lion, wolf, bear, fur seal, bat, pelican, opossum, salmon, shark

  OMNIVORES: frog, sea turtle, whale, alligator

- *Answer to question 2:* The sudden extinction of a group of omnivores in an ecosystem would present a greater problem for the carnivores in the system than for the herbivores. Since carnivores may eat omnivores, they would lose that source of food when the omnivores become extinct. However, herbivores eat only or mostly plants so would be less affected by the disappearance of the omnivores. The herbivores might even increase in population since the extinction of the omnivores would leave more food for them in the ecosystem.

- *Answer to question 3:* The sudden extinction of a population of herbivores in an ecosystem would have immediate and long-lasting effects on the carnivores and omnivores of that ecosystem. Since herbivores eat plants, they serve as the major source of energy for all carnivores and omnivores in a community. These predators could survive for a time by consuming one another, but their future survival would definitely be threatened. In the absence of herbivores who are the primary consumers of an ecosystem, making available to other organisms the solar energy trapped in plants, the carnivores and omnivores would eventually suffer.

woodpecker

frog

lion

turtle

wolf

bear

cow

fur seal

deer

bat

pelican

opossum

sea turtle

salmon

whale

alligator

shark

Name _____ **Date** _____

Life Science

STUDENT HANDOUT–LESSON 36

Basic Principle   Living organisms depend on one another for their survival.

Objective   Classify animals as herbivores, carnivores, or omnivores.

Materials   pictures of living organisms

Procedure

1. Examine, identify, and name the animals in the pictures given to you by your teacher.

2. Discuss the eating habits of each animal with your classmates. Does the animal eat mostly plants? Mostly the meat from other animals? Or, does it eat both plants and the meat from other animals?

3. Animals that eat only or mostly plants are called "herbivores." Animals that eat only or mostly the meat of other animals are called "carnivores." Animals that eat both plants and the meat of other animals are called "omnivores."

4. Classify each animal in the pictures given to you by your teacher as an herbivore, a carnivore, or an omnivore.

5. Next to the name of each animal, list the most common foods in its diet.

6. Answer the questions in the *Observations & Analysis* section.

Observations & Analysis

1. Classify each animal in the pictures given to you by your teacher as an **herbivore**, **carnivore**, or **omnivore**. Next to the name of each animal, list the most common foods in its diet.

HERBIVORES

name   diet

_____

_____

_____

_____

_____

_____

CARNIVORES

name   diet

_____

_____

_____

_____

_____

_____

OMNIVORES

name   diet

_____

_____

_____

name   diet

_____

_____

_____

2. Would the sudden extinction of a group of omnivores present a problem for the herbivores and carnivores in an ecosystem? Explain your answer.

_____

_____

_____

3. Would the sudden extinction of a group of herbivores present a problem for the carnivores and omnivores in an ecosystem? Explain your answer.

_____

_____

_____

Lesson 37: Teacher Preparation

Basic Principle Living organisms depend on one another for their survival.

Competency Students will construct a "food chain" to show that plants, herbivores, carnivores, and omnivores depend on one another for survival.

Materials paper clips, tape, marking pens, scissors, yellow construction paper, magazine pictures of living organisms or the pictures shown here

Procedure Assist students in following the Procedure on STUDENT HANDOUT—LESSON 37.

Observations & Analysis

- *Answer to question 1:* Students will discover that the attachments among the organisms form a web, illustrating the interconnected flow of food energy from the sun to producers then consumers throughout the plant and animal kingdoms.

- *Answer to question 2:* Answers will vary. However, students should describe how the energy flow is disrupted between whole groups of organisms in their "food web."

- *Answer to question 3:* Students will recognize that the animal kingdom becomes disconnected from its primary source of energy: the sun. This type of disaster could eventually result in the extinction of animal life on our planet.

woodpecker

frog

newt

moth

lobster

turtle

spider

shark

wolf

sycamore

grass

fern

de

sea cow

opossum

whale

bat

pelican

salmon

alligator

bear

calf

lion

Name _____ **Date** _____

Life Science

STUDENT HANDOUT–LESSON 37

Basic Principle Living organisms depend on one another for their survival.

Objective Construct a "food chain" to show that plants, herbivores, carnivores, and omnivores depend on one another for survival.

Materials paper clips, tape, marking pens, scissors, yellow construction paper, pictures of living organisms

Procedure

1. Tape a paper clip to the top and bottom of the picture of each plant and animal given to you by your teacher.

2. Identify each living organism as either a producer (for example: a plant) or a consumer (for example: an animal). Identify the herbivores, carnivores, and omnivores in your collection of animals.

3. Cut a circle out of a piece of yellow construction paper to represent the sun. Tape as many paper clips to the sun as you have producers in your picture collection. Energy from the sun radiates to Earth and is stored inside plants in the form of starch.

4. Clip the bottom paper clip of each producer in your collection to the paper clips attached to the sun.

5. Clip the bottom paper clip of each herbivore in your collection to the top clip of different plants.

6. Clip the bottom paper clip of each carnivore in your collection to the top clip of different herbivores.

7. Clip the bottom paper clip of each omnivore in your collection to the top clip of any plant, herbivore, or carnivore.

8. Use extra paper clips in short or long straight chains to clip together carnivores and omnivores that eat one another.

9. Answer the questions in the _Observations & Analysis_ section.

Observations & Analysis

1. How would you describe the model you have made? Does it look like a "straight chain" or more like a "web"?

   _____

   _____

   _____

   _____

2. Remove several plants from the model. Describe how the "energy flow" from the sun to the living organisms in the model has changed.

   _____

   _____

   _____

   _____

3. Describe what would happen in a closed ecosystem if a deadly germ suddenly killed the system's plantlife.

   _____

   _____

   _____

   _____

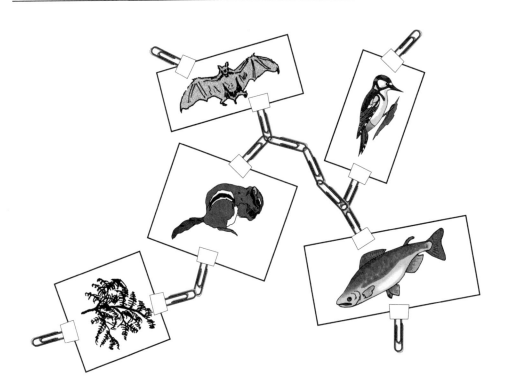

Lesson 38: Teacher Preparation

Basic Principle   Living organisms depend on one another for their survival.

Competency   Students will draw a chart of a "food pyramid" to show how primary and secondary consumers compete for resources in an ecosystem.

Materials   construction paper, scissors, ruler, colored pencils (crayons, or marking pens), glue or tape, magazine pictures of living organisms or the pictures shown here

Procedure   Assist students in following the Procedure on STUDENT HANDOUT—LESSON 38.

Observations & Analysis

- Student charts may vary with respect to the arrangement of second-order and third-order consumers depending on their assessment of each animal's diet. However, students should note that plants are the only producers. First-order consumers include mostly herbivores, such as grazing and seed-eating animals, and plant-eating insects. Second-order consumers mostly include carnivores. Third-order consumers include predominantly omnivores.

- *Answer to question 1:* Answers will vary.

- *Answer to question 2:* Students should conclude that whole groups of animals can be harmfully affected if a common food source becomes unavailable.

woodpecker

frog

newt

earthworm

moth

grasshopper

turtle

spider

shark

wolf

sycamore

grass

fern

de

opossum

whale

bat

pelican

salmon

alligator

bear

calf

lion

172

Name _____ **Date** _____

Life Science

STUDENT HANDOUT–LESSON 38

Basic Principle Living organisms depend on one another for their survival.

Objective Make a chart of a "food pyramid" to show how primary and secondary consumers compete for resources in an ecosystem.

Materials construction paper, scissors, ruler, colored pencils (or crayons or marking pens), glue or tape, pictures of living organisms

Procedure

1. Draw a large triangle, like the one shown here, on a large piece of construction paper. Label the triangle as shown.

2. Look through a magazine. Cut out pictures of plants and animals living in water and on land. Be sure to include the pictures of insects that are important first-order consumers that serve as prey to second-order consumers. (Or use the pictures supplied by your teacher.)

3. Discuss how each type of living organism gets food energy to survive. Producers such as land plants and green algae make their own food by storing the energy of the sun. First-order consumers are usually herbivores that eat mostly plants, algae, and seeds. Second-order consumers are carnivores and omnivores that eat first-order consumers, plants, and seeds.

4. Glue the pictures in their correct location inside the pyramid.

5. Draw arrows to show the different kinds of prey consumed by different kinds of predators.

6. Complete the *Observations & Analysis* section.

Observations & Analysis

1. Make a list of the different consumers that compete for the same foods.

   _____

   _____

   _____

   _____

2. Explain what would happen to the ecosystem if a common food source becomes extinct.

   _____

   _____

   _____

   _____

   _____

   _____

   _____

   _____

   _____

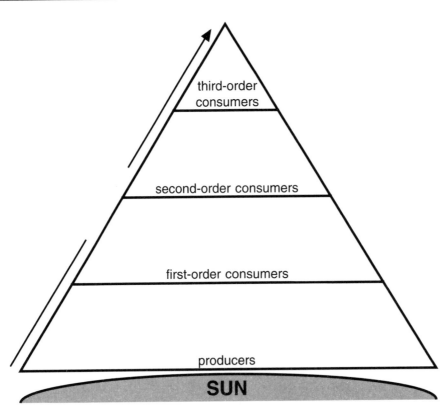

 <u>**Life Science**</u>

Lesson 39: Teacher Preparation

Basic Principle   Living organisms need energy and matter to live and grow.

Competency   Students will show that microorganisms cause decomposition.

Materials   fruits and vegetables, water, sandwich bags, dry yeast, teaspoon, knife, crayons and markers

Procedure

1. Use the drawings to illustrate the different kinds of decomposers that exist in nature. Define a "decomposer" as an organism that breaks down dead matter. Decomposers play a central role in an ecosystem. They free important chemical compounds, such as nitrates locked in excrement which are necessary for plant growth, and recycle those chemicals back into the soil and atmosphere. The three major groups of decomposing organisms include protists, fungi and molds, and bacteria. Many invertebrates, such as earthworms, also assist in decomposing dead matter.

2. Explain that yeast is one of 100,000 different kinds of fungi. They do not have chlorophyll like plants, so they cannot produce their own energy. They must get their food energy from the chemical compounds locked in dead matter. Assist students in following the Procedure on STUDENT HANDOUT—LESSON 39.

Observations & Analysis   *Answer to the question:* Answers will vary. However, students will observe that the foods stored with yeast show considerably more decay than the control group.

MICROSCOPIC PROTISTS

amoeba

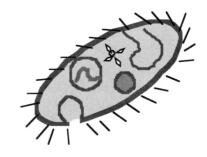

paramecium

FUNGI AND BREAD MOLDS

mushroom

yeast

bread mold

MICROSCOPIC BACTERIA

bacteria

bacteria colony

spirochete

INVERTEBRATES

earthworm

Name _____ **Date** _____

Life Science

STUDENT HANDOUT–LESSON 39

Basic Principle   Living organisms need energy and matter to live and grow.

Objective   Show that microorganisms cause decomposition.

Materials   fruits and vegetables, water, sandwich bags, dry yeast, teaspoon, knife, crayons and markers

Procedure

1. Gather samples of fruits and vegetables such as a banana, an apple, a pear, a carrot, a tomato, celery, and lettuce leaves.

2. Cut two small pieces of each kind of fruit and vegetable.

3. Place each small sample inside a sandwich bag.

4. Add a half teaspoon of water to each bag.

5. Add a half teaspoon of dry yeast to one sample of each kind of fruit and vegetable.

6. Seal all bags. Mark the bags containing the yeast with the letter "M." The "M" stands for the word "microorganism." There are thousands of different kinds of microorganisms like yeast, such as bacteria, molds, and fungi. Microorganisms survive by breaking down the nutrients of other organisms and feeding on them. This breakdown is called "decomposition."

7. Examine each bag after one week.

8. Complete the *Observations & Analysis* section.

Observations & Analysis   Label, draw, and color the fruit and vegetable remains in each bag after one week.

Which fruits and vegetables showed the fastest decomposition?

_____

_____

_____

_____

 **Life Science**

Lesson 40: Teacher Preparation

Basic Principle   Living organisms depend on one another for survival.

Competency   Students will discuss the eating habits of insects to explain how they help recycle matter from dead plants and animals to living organisms.

Materials   food pyramid chart made in LESSON 38, magazine pictures of living organisms or the pictures shown here

Procedure

1. While many insects are considered pests, they all play a role in recycling natural resources throughout the environment. There are more than one million species known and thousands more are discovered every year.

2. Assist students in following the Procedure on STUDENT HANDOUT—LESSON 40.

Observations & Analysis

- *Answer to question 1:* Answers will vary. However, students should conclude that insects live by ingesting dead matter or by eating other insects.

- *Answer to question 2:* Earthworms, beetles, and flies get their nutrients from feeding on decomposing matter.

- *Answer to question 3:* These summary diagrams will vary, but should show how energy from the sun is processed and stored by plant producers and then consumed by first-order, second-order, and third-order animal consumers. Dead plants and animals are then consumed by decomposers who recycle valuable nutrients back into an ecosystem.

INSECTS

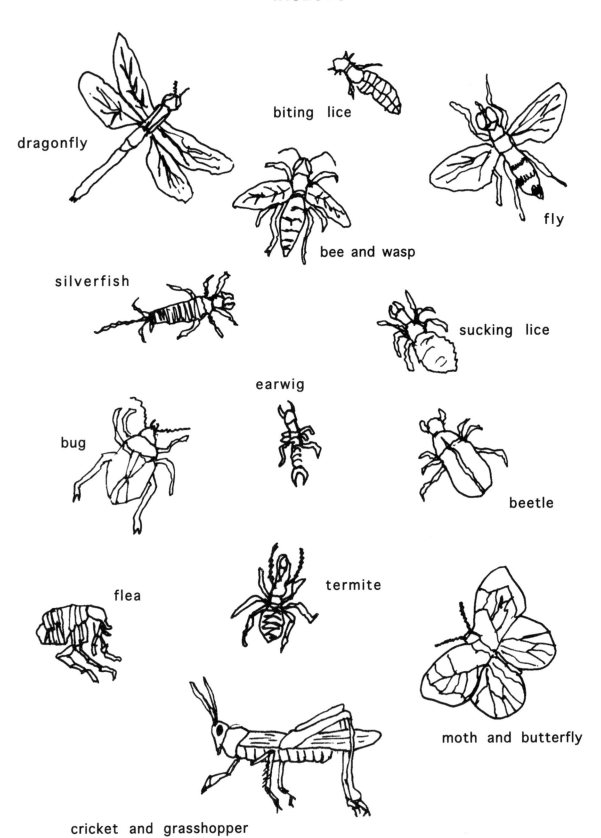

dragonfly

biting lice

fly

bee and wasp

silverfish

sucking lice

earwig

bug

beetle

flea

termite

moth and butterfly

cricket and grasshopper

Life Science

STUDENT HANDOUT–LESSON 40

Basic Principle   Living organisms depend on one another for their survival.

Objective   Discuss the eating habits of insects to explain how they help recycle matter from dead plants and animals to living organisms.

Materials   food pyramid chart made in LESSON 38

Procedure

1. Examine the "food pyramid chart" that you made in Lesson 38. Focus on the eating habits of the insects you included in your chart.

2. Have a discussion with your classmates about the eating habits of these insects. In addition to the living plants and other insects commonly eaten by these organisms, consider the food sources of earthworms, beetles, and flies.

3. Complete the *Observations & Analysis* section.

Observations & Analysis

1. List the food sources of the insects on your chart as well as the food sources of insects such as earthworms, beetles, and flies.

   _____

   _____

   _____

   _____

2. Do earthworms, beetles, and flies eat living organisms? Or, do they get their nutrients from decomposing matter?

   _____

   _____

   _____

3. Draw a diagram with labels and arrows that shows how energy and nutrients are recycled in an ecosystem. Include the sun, producers, first-order consumers, second-order consumers, third-order consumers, and decomposers such as bacteria, molds, fungi, and yeast.

 **Life Science**

Lesson 41: Teacher Preparation

Basic Principle   Living organisms depend on living and nonliving resources in the environment.

Competency   Students will list the living and nonliving resources in different ecosystems.

Materials   magazine pictures of different ecosystems such as forests, meadows, pastures, mountains, ponds, and streams

Procedure   Assist students in following the Procedure on STUDENT HANDOUT—LESSON 41.

Observations & Analysis   *Answer to the question:* Answers will vary. However, students should mention that air and water are the primary nonliving resources essential for the survival of all living organisms on our planet. Rocks, soil, and dead plants provide warmth and shelter, giving protection against the weather and natural predators.

Name _____ **Date** _____

Life Science

STUDENT HANDOUT–LESSON 41

Basic Principle   Living organisms depend on living and nonliving resources in the environment.

Objective   List the living and nonliving resources in different ecosystems.

Materials   magazine pictures of different ecosystems such as forests, meadows, pastures, mountains, ponds, and streams

Procedure

1. Choose any two of the pictures provided by your teacher.

2. Make a diagram showing the positions of as many different kinds of plants and animals that live in each ecosystem shown.

3. Add to the diagram by showing the nonliving resources that help the living organisms to survive, such as air, water, and minerals. Don't forget to include the materials that provide the living organisms with shelter and protection from predators.

4. Complete the *Observations & Analysis* section.

```
┌─────────────────────────────────────────────┐
│                 ECOSYSTEM #1                 │
│                                              │
│                                              │
│                                              │
│                                              │
│                                              │
│                                              │
│                                              │
└─────────────────────────────────────────────┘
```

```
┌─────────────────────────────────────────────┐
│                 ECOSYSTEM #2                 │
│                                              │
│                                              │
│                                              │
│                                              │
│                                              │
│                                              │
│                                              │
└─────────────────────────────────────────────┘
```

Observations & Analysis   Explain how the survival of each living organism would be threatened if one or more of the nonliving resources were not present.

_____

_____

_____

_____

_____

_____

_____

Lesson 42: Teacher Preparation

Basic Principle Living organisms depend on living and nonliving resources in the environment.

Competency Students will discuss how the survival of living organisms depends on nonliving resources in the environment.

Materials classmates

Procedure

1. Prompt discussion with a review of the essential nonliving resources in an ecosystem: the sun, air, water, rocks, soil, and decaying matter.
2. Assist students in following the Procedure on STUDENT HANDOUT—LESSON 42.

Essay Students' essays should include a description of the nonliving resources in an ecosystem: the sun, air, water, rocks, soil, and decaying matter. They should discuss how their chosen animal acquires and uses these resources.

Life Science

STUDENT HANDOUT–LESSON 42

Basic Principle   Living organisms depend on living and nonliving resources in the environment.

Objective   Discuss how the survival of living organisms depends on nonliving resources in the environment.

Materials   classmates

Procedure

1. Write the name of your favorite forest animal in the "Notes" section below.

2. List the living and nonliving resources your animal needs to survive.

3. Write a brief short story describing a day in the life of your animal. Describe where the animal lives, how it keeps dry and warm, where and how it finds food and water.

4. Read your story to a group of classmates.

5. Allow your classmates to discuss your story. Write down any suggestions they make that will help you to improve your story.

Notes   My favorite forest animal is the _____.

My animal will require the following living and nonliving resources to survive a day in the forest:

_____

_____

_____

_____

_____

_____

_____

A DAY IN THE LIFE OF MY FAVORITE FOREST ANIMAL

_____

_____

_____

_____

_____

_____

_____

_____

_____

_____

_____

_____

_____

_____

WAYS I CAN IMPROVE MY STORY

_____

_____

_____

_____

 **Life Science**

Lesson 43: Teacher Preparation

Basic Principle   How well adapted organisms are to their environment determines how well they survive.

Competency   Students will show that for any particular environment some kinds of organisms survive well, some survive less well, and some cannot survive at all.

Materials   bowl, paper cups, toothpicks, tweezers, straws, spoons, uncooked macaroni

Procedure

1. Begin discussion by asking students to look around the room and observe the individual differences between themselves and their classmates. Point out that all organisms are adapted to their environment in ways that help them to survive. Since the English economist Thomas Malthus (1766–1834) published an article in 1798 about how populations continue to increase in number as long as natural resources are available, scientists have known that organisms compete for survival because natural resources tend to be limited. The English naturalist Charles Darwin (1809–1882) based much of the theory of evolution by means of natural selection on the ideas of Malthus. According to Darwin's Theory of Evolution, organisms compete in a "struggle for survival" in which some kinds of organisms survive well, some survive less well, and some cannot survive at all.

2. Assist students in following the Procedure on STUDENT HANDOUT—LESSON 43.

Observations & Analysis

- *Result Record:* Results will vary depending on how skillful each student is at using the "adaptive tool" he or she is given.

- *Answer to question 2:* Answers will vary. However, students' responses should be logical and well defended.

- *Answer to question 3:* Answers will vary. However, students' responses should be logical and well defended.

- *Answer to question 4:* Students should conclude that for any particular environment, some kinds of organisms survive well, some survive less well, and some cannot survive at all.

Name _____ **Date** _____

Life Science

STUDENT HANDOUT–LESSON 43

Basic Principle   How well adapted organisms are to their environment determines how well they survive.

Objective   Show that for any particular environment some kind of animals survive well, some survive less well, and some cannot survive at all.

Materials   bowl, paper cups, toothpicks, tweezers, straws, spoons, uncooked macaroni

Procedure

1. Fill a bowl with uncooked macaroni and place it in the center of your group.

2. Your teacher has given you a paper cup containing one of the following items: a straw, a spoon, a pair of toothpicks, or pair of tweezers.

3. When the teacher says "GO!" you may use that "tool"—and only that tool—to transfer macaroni from the bowl to your paper cup. DO NOT PICK UP ANY OF THE MACARONI WITH YOUR FINGERS ALONE. DO NOT INTERFERE WITH THE EFFORT OF OTHERS!

4. When the bowl is empty, record the number of macaroni in each cup.

5. Complete the *Observations & Analysis* section.

Observations & Analysis

1. Record the number of macaroni "consumed" by:

   the straw _____   the spoon _____

   the pair of toothpicks _____   the pair of tweezers _____

2. Which set of tools was most successful at consuming the macaroni? Suggest some kinds of foods that this tool might have trouble consuming.

   _____

   _____

   _____

   _____

3. Which set of tools was least successful at consuming the macaroni? Suggest some kinds of foods that this tool might have less trouble consuming.

   _____

   _____

   _____

   _____

4. Explain how the adaptations of an organism determine how well it will survive in a particular environment.

   _____

   _____

   _____

   _____

   _____

   _____

   _____

   _____

   _____

   _____

   _____

   _____

 **Life Science**

Lesson 44: Teacher Preparation

Basic Principle   Living organisms depend on one another for survival.

Competency   Students will show that many microorganisms do not cause disease and can be beneficial to other living organisms.

Materials   powdered yeast, sugar, 2 plastic water bottles (about 500 mL each), spoon, 2 balloons, marking pen

Procedure

1. Review the results of the experiment performed in LESSON 39 and the assortment of protists, fungi, molds, and bacteria that live in our environment. Point out that penicillin, a drug made from the mold *penicillium*, is used as an antibiotic to kill germs. Point out that yeast is used in the baking of cakes and breads.

2. Assist students in following the Procedure on STUDENT HANDOUT—LESSON 44.

3. Remind students that yeast is a fungus that feeds on dead matter. Yeast derives its energy by changing the sugar stored in dead plants into carbon dioxide gas and energy. The carbon dioxide bubbles produced in this experiment cause the balloon to inflate. For this reason, yeast is used in baking. The yeast produces carbon dioxide that causes dough to rise in an oven during the baking of bread.

Observations & Analysis

- *Drawings:* Drawings will vary. However, the balloon on the bottle containing a mixture of water, yeast, and sugar should show an increasing number of bubbles as the balloon inflates. The balloon covering the control bottle containing only sugar and water will not inflate.

- *Answer to question 2:* Observations will vary depending upon the amount of carbon dioxide produced in the bottle containing yeast and sugar. However, students should note that the bottle containing this mixture also contains bubbles that inflate the balloon.

- *Answer to question 3:* Students should conclude that a chemical reaction among the water, yeast, and sugar has produced carbon dioxide bubbles. Carbon dioxide bubbles produced during any baking process that uses yeast will make the food "fluffy."

RESULTS AT DAY 3

balloons

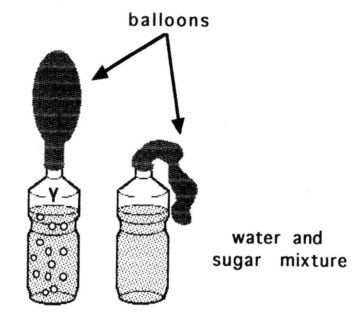

water, yeast, and sugar mixture

water and sugar mixture

plastic bottles

Name _____ **Date** _____

Life Science
STUDENT HANDOUT–LESSON 44

Basic Principle   Living organisms depend on one another for their survival.

Objective   Many microorganisms do not cause disease and can be beneficial to other living organisms.

Materials   powdered yeast, sugar, 2 plastic water bottles (about 500 mL each), spoon, 2 balloons, marking pen

Procedure

1. Fill two plastic water bottles halfway with warm water. Make sure the water is warm, not hot.

2. Add one teaspoon of sugar to each bottle.

3. Add one teaspoon of powdered yeast to only one of the bottles. Use a marking pen to label that bottle with a "Y."

4. Cap the bottles and gently swirl their contents to be sure they are mixed.

5. Uncap the bottles and fill them to their necks with more warm water.

6. Stretch the mouth of a balloon over the mouth of each bottle to seal them.

7. Store the mixtures in a dark and warm place.

8. Observe the bottles every day for several days and complete the *Observations & Analysis* section.

bottle containing
mixture of water,
sugar, and
powdered yeast

bottle containing
mixture of water
and sugar

Observations & Analysis

1. Draw a picture of your balloon-sealed bottles every day for three days.

Day 1	Day 2	Day 3

2. Describe your observations.

_____

_____

_____

_____

_____

3. Explain your observations.

_____

_____

_____

_____

_____

_____

_____

_____

 **Life Science**

Lesson 45: Teacher Preparation

Basic Principle   Living organisms depend on one another for survival.

Competency   Students will show that many plants depend on insects and animals for pollination and seed dispersal.

Materials   magazine pictures of flowers and bees, fruit and berry trees, and forest animals

Procedure

1. Explain to students that flowering plants reproduce by spreading their seeds to areas where the soil is moist and rich with nutrients. Seed dispersal can be accomplished in a number of ways. Wind and rain can spread seeds throughout an ecosystem. But insects, such as bees, and animals, such as deer and other herbivores, help a lot in the process.

2. Define the term "pollen" as a tiny grain of reproductive material that contains the male part of a flowering plant's genetic instructions for plant growth. Define the term "pollination" as the process by which plants produce fertilized seeds containing both the male and female genetic instructions for plant growth. Define the term "seed" as the reproductive structure of a plant that contains genetic material from both the male and female parts of a flowering plant.

3. Assist students in following the Procedure on STUDENT HANDOUT—LESSON 45.

Observations & Analysis

- Definitions should be written as given above.

- *Drawings:* Drawings will vary. However, the students' "BEES AND POLLINATION" illustrations should show bees transferring pollen grains attached to their bodies from one flowering plant to another as the bees go in search of sweet nectar to eat. The students' "ANIMALS AND SEED DISPERSAL" illustrations should show animals eating fruits and berries, then depositing their seed-carrying feces in another part of the ecosystem.

- *Answer to the question:* Students should mention that plants would have trouble reproducing if their seeds were not spread to places where the soil is moist and rich with nutrients. Bees and other forest animals assist plants in accomplishing this goal.

Name _____ **Date** _____

Life Science

STUDENT HANDOUT–LESSON 45

Basic Principle   Living organisms depend on one another for their survival.

Objective   Many plants depend on insects and animals for pollination and seed dispersal.

Materials   magazine pictures of flowers and bees, fruit and berry trees, and forest animals

Procedure

1. Write the definition of each of the following terms as directed by your teacher: pollen, pollination, seed.

2. Examine the pictures provided by your teacher.

3. Draw a diagram to show how bees can transfer pollen from flower to flower.

4. Draw a diagram where forest animals find, eat, and digest fruit and berries. Then describe how they transport the seeds of these foods to other parts of their ecosystem.

5. Complete the *Observations & Analysis* section.

Definitions

pollen: _____

_____

pollination: _____

_____

seed: _____

_____

BEES AND POLLINATION	ANIMALS AND SEED DISPERSAL

Observations & Analysis   Explain how the survival of plants depends upon the presence of bees and forest animals in their ecosystem.

_____

_____

_____

_____

_____

_____

FOURTH-GRADE LEVEL

Life Science

PRACTICE TEST

Life Science

PRACTICE TEST

Directions: Use the Answer Sheet to darken the letter of the choice that best answers each question.

1. What will the leaves of a green plant do when it is left in the sun for a day?

   (A) The leaves will wilt.

   (B) The leaves will point toward the soil.

   (C) The leaves will point toward the sun.

   (D) The leaves will point north.

   (E) The leaves will change color.

2. What will happen to the leaves of a green plant that is placed in the dark for several days?

   (A) The leaves will die.

   (B) The leaves will point toward the ground.

   (C) The leaves will swell.

   (D) The leaves will point north.

   (E) The leaves will grow healthy.

3. Which substance is produced by a healthy plant?

   (A) nitrogen

   (B) water

   (C) carbon dioxide

   (D) starch

   (E) minerals

4. Which of the following foods has the most starch?

   (A) milk

   (B) eggs

   (C) potato

   (D) meat

   (E) fish

5. Which of the following living organisms is a "producer"?

   (A) bacteria

   (B) earthworm

   (C) grass

   (D) bumblebee

   (E) mouse

6. Which of the following living organisms is *not* a "consumer"?

   (A) ant

   (B) cow

   (C) lobster

   (D) sunflower

   (E) human being

7. Which of the following living organisms is a "herbivore"?

   (A) mushroom

   (B) fern

   (C) deer

   (D) lion

   (E) bear

8. Which of the following living organisms is *not* a "carnivore"?

    (A) sheep

    (B) snake

    (C) hawk

    (D) cat

    (E) bear

9. Which of the following living organisms is an "omnivore"?

    (A) elephant

    (B) whale

    (C) eagle

    (D) human being

    (E) pine tree

10. Which of the following best describes the flow of energy in an ecosystem?

    (A) sun ➡ cow ➡ grass

    (B) sun ➡ grass ➡ cow

    (C) grass ➡ sun ➡ cow

    (D) cow ➡ sun ➡ grass

    (E) cow ➡ grass ➡ sun

11. Which type of living organism helps to return soil nutrients to the ecosystem?

    (A) herbivore

    (B) carnivore

    (C) omnivore

    (D) decomposer

    (E) primary consumer

12. Which of the following living organisms helps to break down dead matter and return nutrients to the soil?

    (A) bacteria

    (B) earthworm

    (C) mushroom

    (D) yeast

    (E) All of the above perform this function.

13. Which of the following best describes the eating habits of an insect?

    (A) producer

    (B) decomposer

    (C) first-order consumer

    (D) second-order consumer

    (E) third-order consumer

14. Which of the following is *not* a nonliving resource of the environment?

    (A) fungus

    (B) water

    (C) air

    (D) minerals

    (E) the sun

15. Which of the following most affects how well an organism will survive?

    (A) the organism's size

    (B) the organism's weight

    (C) the organism's shelter

    (D) the organism's color

    (E) the organism's adaptations to its environment

16. Which of the following is true?

    (A) All microorganisms are dangerous.

    (B) All microorganisms are producers.

    (C) All microorganisms need direct sunlight to survive.

    (D) Many microorganisms benefit people.

    (E) Many microorganisms cannot survive in plants.

17. Which of the following organisms helps to spread seeds around the environment?

    (A) gorilla

    (B) cow

    (C) deer

    (D) raccoon

    (E) all of the above

18. Which of the following organisms helps to pollinate flowering plants?

    (A) bee

    (B) wasp

    (C) moth

    (D) butterfly

    (E) all of the above

Matching: Choose the letter of the term that best matches its definition. (Use the Answer Sheet.)

    (A) producer

    (B) consumer

    (C) herbivore

    (D) carnivore

    (E) omnivore

19. an organism that eats mostly animals

20. an organism that eats mostly plants

21. an organism that makes its own starch

22. an organism that feeds on other organisms

Matching: Choose the letter of the term or phrase that best describes the organism's place in the food pyramid. (Use the Answer Sheet.)

    (A) producer

    (B) first-order consumer

    (C) second-order consumer

    (D) third-order consumer

    (E) decomposer

23. mushroom

24. sheep

25. hawk

Life Science

PRACTICE TEST: ANSWER SHEET

Name _____ **Date** _____ **Period** _____

Darken the circle above the letter that best answers the question.

#	A	B	C	D	E		#	A	B	C	D	E
1.	○	○	○	○	○		14.	○	○	○	○	○
2.	○	○	○	○	○		15.	○	○	○	○	○
3.	○	○	○	○	○		16.	○	○	○	○	○
4.	○	○	○	○	○		17.	○	○	○	○	○
5.	○	○	○	○	○		18.	○	○	○	○	○
6.	○	○	○	○	○		19.	○	○	○	○	○
7.	○	○	○	○	○		20.	○	○	○	○	○
8.	○	○	○	○	○		21.	○	○	○	○	○
9.	○	○	○	○	○		22.	○	○	○	○	○
10.	○	○	○	○	○		23.	○	○	○	○	○
11.	○	○	○	○	○		24.	○	○	○	○	○
12.	○	○	○	○	○		25.	○	○	○	○	○
13.	○	○	○	○	○							

Life Science

KEY TO PRACTICE TEST

1. A ○ B ○ C ● D ○ E ○
2. A ● B ○ C ○ D ○ E ○
3. A ○ B ○ C ○ D ● E ○
4. A ○ B ○ C ● D ○ E ○
5. A ○ B ○ C ● D ○ E ○
6. A ○ B ○ C ○ D ● E ○
7. A ○ B ○ C ● D ○ E ○
8. A ● B ○ C ○ D ○ E ○
9. A ○ B ○ C ○ D ● E ○
10. A ○ B ● C ○ D ○ E ○
11. A ○ B ○ C ○ D ● E ○
12. A ○ B ○ C ○ D ○ E ●
13. A ○ B ○ C ● D ○ E ○

14. A ● B ○ C ○ D ○ E ○
15. A ○ B ○ C ○ D ○ E ●
16. A ○ B ○ C ○ D ● E ○
17. A ○ B ○ C ○ D ○ E ●
18. A ○ B ○ C ○ D ○ E ●
19. A ○ B ○ C ○ D ● E ○
20. A ○ B ○ C ● D ○ E ○
21. A ● B ○ C ○ D ○ E ○
22. A ○ B ● C ○ D ○ E ○
23. A ○ B ○ C ○ D ○ E ●
24. A ○ B ● C ○ D ○ E ○
25. A ○ B ○ C ● D ○ E ○

Section IV: Earth Science

LESSONS AND ACTIVITIES

Lesson 46 Students will define terms used to describe the methods of rock formation. They will use these terms to complete a diagram describing the rock cycle.

Lesson 47 Students will tell the difference among igneous, sedimentary, and metamorphic rocks by examining their properties and discussing their methods of formation (the rock cycle).

Lesson 48 Students will show that sedimentary rocks contain carbonates, a substance found commonly in the shells of sea creatures.

Lesson 49 Students will show that the size of rock particles can affect how quickly rocks are broken down.

Lesson 50 Students will construct paper models of different kinds of rock crystals.

Lesson 51 Students will grow sodium bicarbonate crystals.

Lesson 52 Students will identify the hardness of minerals using the Mohs Scale of Hardness.

Lesson 53 Students will show how the formation of cave stalagmites and stalactites occurs.

Lesson 54 Students will demonstrate how wind changes sand formations in deserts and beaches.

Lesson 55 Students will demonstrate how water changes sand and soil formations.

Lesson 56 Students will show that water expands when freezing.

Lesson 57 Students will show that freezing water can break hard materials such as metals and rocks.

Lesson 58 Students will show how the Earth's crustal plates move about on the surface of our planet.

Lesson 59 Students will show how the Earth's crustal plates press together to form mountain ranges and folds.

Lesson 60 Students will show how the pressure builds up in volcanoes, resulting in their periodic eruptions.

Lesson 61 Students will show how landforms are eroded by abrasion.

Lesson 62 Students will show how different kinds of soil affect the flow of water through Earth landforms.

EARTH SCIENCE PRACTICE TEST

 **Earth Science**

Lesson 46: Teacher Preparation

Basic Principle   The properties of rocks and minerals reflect the processes that formed them.

Competency   Students will define terms used to describe the methods of rock formation. They will use these terms to complete a diagram describing the rock cycle.

Materials   igneous (e.g., quartz, granite, obsidian, pitchstone, perlite, pumice, tuff), sedimentary (e.g., conglomerate, breccia, coquina, sandstone, limestone, siltstone, dolomite), metamorphic (e.g., gneiss, schist, phyllite, slate, marble, serpentine, soapstone, talc) rocks

Procedure   Display a variety of rocks. Write the *Observations & Definitions* section on the board. Assist students in defining the TYPES OF ROCK and geological FORMATION PROCESSES listed by completing the sentences on STUDENT HANDOUT—LESSON 46. Help them to classify each rock as igneous, sedimentary, or metamorphic by examining the features of each rock. Give them time to complete the diagram of The Rock Cycle on STUDENT HANDOUT—LESSON 46 using the terms for each formation process.

Observations & Definitions

TYPES OF ROCK

magma: melted volcanic matter

igneous: crystallized volcanic matter

sedimentary: weathered, eroded, compacted, layered, cracked or fractured matter

metamorphic: heated and pressurized matter

FORMATION PROCESSES

melting (i.e., formation of liquified rock)

crystallization (i.e., formation of crystals having the same mineral content)

weathering, erosion, compacting or layering, fracturing, cementation (i.e., formation of rock debris by physical destruction)

metamorphism (i.e., formation of new minerals by chemical change due to slow heating and pressurization)

THE ROCK CYCLE

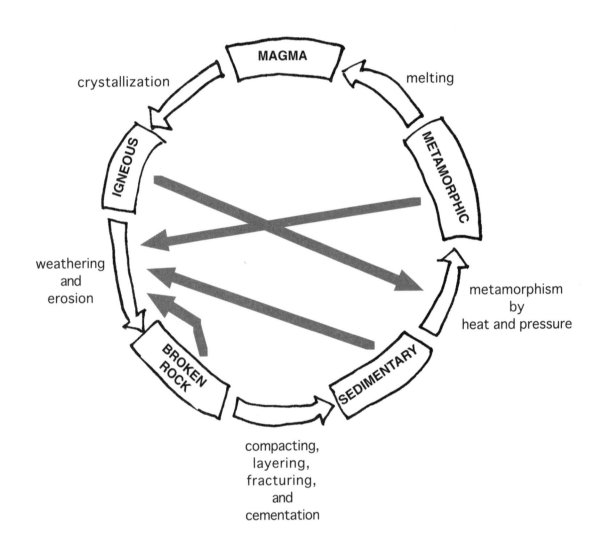

Name _____ **Date** _____

Earth Science

STUDENT HANDOUT–LESSON 46

Basic Principle   The properties of rocks and minerals reflect the processes that formed them.

Objective   Define terms used to describe the methods of rock formation. Use these terms to complete a diagram that explains the rock cycle.

Materials   pen or pencil

Procedure

1. Examine the rocks displayed by your teacher.

2. As your teacher shows you each rock, complete the sentences below using the terms listed on the board. These terms are used to describe the different ways rocks are formed.

3. Complete the diagram using these terms.

Observations & Definitions

Magma is _____

Magma is formed by _____

_____

Igneous rock is _____

Igneous rock is formed by _____

_____

_____

_____

Sedimentary rock is _____

Sedimentary rock is formed by _____

_____

_____

_____

_____

Metamorphic rock is _____

Metamorphic rock is formed by _____

_____

_____

_____

THE ROCK CYCLE

Directions: The diagram shows how rocks are transformed from one type to another. Write the name of the formation process that changes each type of rock next to the appropriate white arrow.

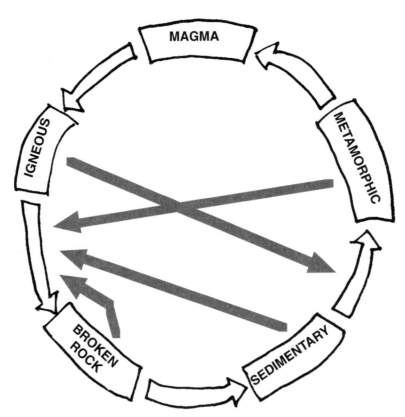

 **Earth Science**

Lesson 47: Teacher Preparation

Basic Principle   The properties of rocks and minerals reflect the processes that formed them.

Competency   Students will tell the difference among igneous, sedimentary, and metamorphic rocks by examining their properties and discussing their methods of formation (the rock cycle).

Materials   igneous (e.g., quartz, granite, obsidian, pitchstone, perlite, pumice, tuff), sedimentary (e.g., conglomerate, breccia, coquina, sandstone, limestone, siltstone, dolomite), metamorphic (e.g., gneiss, schist, phyllite, slate, marble, serpentine, soapstone, talc) rocks

Procedure   Prepare for the lesson by numbering and labeling with tape a sampling of rocks so that you have a key to the identity of each one. Distribute rocks so that each group of students has two igneous, two sedimentary, and two metamorphic rocks. Instruct students to draw each rock and discuss the formation processes that might have formed each rock. Have them classify the rocks as either igneous, sedimentary, or metamorphic using the diagram they completed on STUDENT HANDOUT—LESSON 46.

Observations & Analysis   Student answers will vary depending upon the rocks they are given. Accept any logical conclusions that demonstrate their understanding of the formation processes occurring in the rock cycle. Point out that professional geologists do not rely on visual observations alone. They test the physical and chemical properties of rocks using a variety of scientific instruments and techniques. Geologists identify and classify rocks according to their mineral (i.e., chemical crystalline) content, their relative hardness, and their density.

ROCK IDENTIFICATION KEY

Rock Number	Specific name (e.g., quartz, schist, slate)	Classification (e.g., igneous, sedimentary, metamorphic)
_____	_____	_____
_____	_____	_____
_____	_____	_____
_____	_____	_____
_____	_____	_____
_____	_____	_____
_____	_____	_____
_____	_____	_____
_____	_____	_____
_____	_____	_____
_____	_____	_____
_____	_____	_____
_____	_____	_____
_____	_____	_____
_____	_____	_____
_____	_____	_____
_____	_____	_____
_____	_____	_____
_____	_____	_____
_____	_____	_____
_____	_____	_____
_____	_____	_____
_____	_____	_____
_____	_____	_____
_____	_____	_____
_____	_____	_____
_____	_____	_____
_____	_____	_____
_____	_____	_____
_____	_____	_____
_____	_____	_____

Name _____   **Date** _____

Earth Science

STUDENT HANDOUT–LESSON 47

Basic Principle   The properties of rocks and minerals reflect the processes that formed them.

Objective   Classify different rocks as igneous, sedimentary, or metamorphic by examining their properties and discussing their method of formation.

Materials   2 igneous rocks, 2 sedimentary rocks, 2 metamorphic rocks, colored pencils

Procedure

1. Examine and draw each rock given to your group.
2. Discuss the formation process that might have formed each rock.
3. Classify each rock as igneous, sedimentary, or metamorphic. Give the reasons for your decision in each case.

Observations & Analysis

I classified Rock #_____ as _____ because _____

_____

_____

I classified Rock #_____ as _____ because _____

_____

_____

I classified Rock #_____ as _____ because _____

_____

_____

I classified Rock #_____ as _____ because _____

_____

_____

I classified Rock #_____ as _____ because _____

_____

_____

I classified Rock #_____ as _____ because _____

_____

_____

Rock #_____	Rock #_____
Rock #_____	Rock #_____
Rock #_____	Rock #_____

Lesson 48: Teacher Preparation

Basic Principle   The properties of rocks and minerals reflect the processes that formed them.

Competency   Students will show that sedimentary rocks contain carbonates, a substance found commonly in the shells of sea creatures.

Materials   protective goggles, sedimentary rocks, magnifying glass, eyedropper, small beaker, mild hydrochloric acid

Procedure

1. Prepare an extremely mild solution of 1 molar hydrochloric acid or purchase some from a laboratory supply house.

2. Test your samples using the chart shown here. Then display numbered sedimentary rocks (e.g., sandstone, limestone, or any of the many cemented conglomerates).

3. Explain to students that sedimentary rocks are formed by the erosion and weathering of other rocks followed by the compacting and cementing of rock bits and pieces. Some sedimentary rocks are simply clumps of sediment that have been cemented together. Others are pressed or compacted into layers giving the rock a "stratified" appearance. Still others contain the remains or impressions of actual seashells. Explain that shells are made of calcium carbonate, the same compound that makes up the mineral calcite. Point out that seashells belong to a biological group of animals called mollusks. Mollusks absorb carbon dioxide from the air or water to make their hard shells out of calcium carbonate. Pouring acid on calcium carbonate splits the calcium carbonate molecule into calcium oxide and carbon dioxide. The carbon dioxide gas bubbles back into the atmosphere. The "acid test" can be used to identify the presence of calcium carbonate in rocks that once contained the remains of living creatures.

4. **WARN STUDENTS ABOUT THE HAZARDOUS EFFECTS OF ACIDS AND MAKE SURE THEY WEAR GOGGLES DURING THE EXPERIMENT.**

5. Assist students in completing the activity on STUDENT HANDOUT—LESSON 48.

Observations & Analysis   Students' answers will vary. However, samples containing the remains or impressions of seashells will produce the most bubbles.

ROCK IDENTIFICATION KEY

Rock Number	Rock Type (e.g., sandstone, limestone, etc.)	Pre-Lesson Acid Test Did the sample contain carbonates? (Y/N)

Name _____ **Date** _____

Earth Science

STUDENT HANDOUT–LESSON 48

Basic Principle   The properties of rocks and minerals reflect the processes that formed them.

Objective   Show that sedimentary rocks contain carbonates, a substance found commonly in the shells of sea creatures.

Materials   protective goggles, sedimentary rocks, magnifying glass, eyedropper, small beaker, mild hydrochloric acid

Procedure

1. Use a magnifying glass to examine each rock sample given to you by your teacher.

2. Write a brief comment in the *Observations & Analysis* section about the appearance of each sample of sedimentary rock.

3. **PUT ON PROTECTIVE GOGGLES. YOU MUST WEAR GOGGLES WHEN USING ACID!**

4. Use the eyedropper to put a drop of mild hydrochloric acid on the rock. Observe with the magnifying glass what happens. Hydrochloric acid produces a chemical reaction with carbonate-containing compounds. The product of the reaction is carbon dioxide gas.

5. Write "yes" if carbonate is probably present in the rock sample. Write "no" if it is not.

Observations & Analysis   Write a brief comment about the appearance of each sample of sedimentary rock. Is the sample layered or cemented? Does it contain the imprints of seashells or other organisms? Record how the sample reacted to the drop of hydrochloric acid. Write "yes" if you think carbonate is present in the rock sample. Write "no" if you think it is not.

rock sample	appearance	carbonate present
_____	_____	_____
_____	_____	_____
_____	_____	_____
_____	_____	_____
_____	_____	_____

Why do you think carbonates were present in the rock samples?

_____

_____

_____

_____

_____

Lesson 49: Teacher Preparation

Basic Principle   Rock size and composition determine how quickly rocks are broken down.

Competency   Students will show that the size of rock particles can affect how quickly rocks are broken down.

Materials   protective goggles, chalk, paper towel, hammer, 2 small bowls or petri dishes, eyedropper, mild hydrochloric acid

Procedure

1. Prepare an extremely mild solution of 1 molar hydrochloric acid or purchase some from a laboratory supply house.

2. Test your samples using the chart given here. Then display numbered sedimentary rocks (e.g., sandstone, limestone, or any of the many cemented conglomerates).

3. Remind students that seashells found in some sedimentary rocks contain calcium carbonate, the same compound used to make blackboard chalk. Review the effects of pouring mild acid on calcium carbonate. The acid splits the calcium carbonate molecule into calcium oxide and carbon dioxide bubbles.

4. **WARN STUDENTS ABOUT THE HAZARDOUS EFFECTS OF ACIDS AND MAKE SURE THEY WEAR GOGGLES DURING THE EXPERIMENT.**

5. Assist students in completing the activity on STUDENT HANDOUT—LESSON 49. Explain why more bubbles of carbon dioxide were produced in the powdered sample. Broken rock exposes a greater surface to the environment that can be affected by mechanical or chemical action.

Observations & Analysis

- *Answer to question 1:* Numerous bubbles were produced during the reaction.
- *Answer to question 2:* Fewer bubbles were produced during the reaction.
- *Answer to question 3:* Acid reacts with carbonates in the rock to produce carbon dioxide bubbles.
- *Answer to question 4:* Yes. The powdered sample produced more bubbles because broken rock exposes a greater surface to the environment. A greater surface area is affected more by mechanical or chemical action.

HOW SURFACE AREA DETERMINES THE BREAKDOWN OF ROCKS

broken rock exposing
a large amount of surface area

chunks of rock exposing
a lesser amount of surface area

surface area

surface area

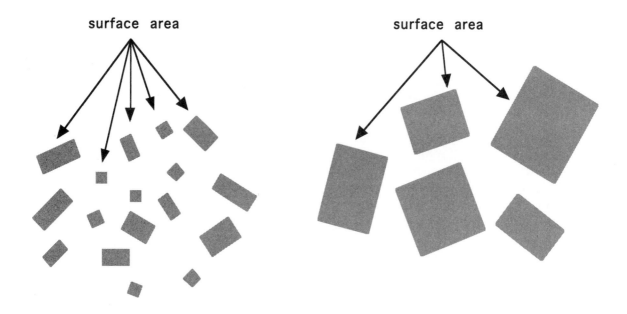

Name _____ **Date** _____

Earth Science

STUDENT HANDOUT–LESSON 49

Basic Principle   Rock size and composition determine how quickly rocks are broken down.

Objective   Show that the size of rock particles can affect how quickly rocks are broken down.

Materials   protective goggles, chalk, paper towel, hammer, 2 small bowls or petri dishes, eyedropper, mild hydrochloric acid

Procedure

1. Break the samples of chalk into small sections.
2. Wrap one half of the chalk chips in a paper towel.
3. Use a hammer to gently pound the chips into powder.
4. Pour the powder into one of the small bowls or petri dishes.
5. Place the remainder of the chips into the other small bowl or petri dish.
6. **PUT ON PROTECTIVE GOGGLES. YOU MUST WEAR GOGGLES WHEN USING ACID!**
7. Add a full eyedropper of the mild hydrochloric acid to each sample of chalk. Chalk is made of calcium carbonate.
8. Complete the *Observations & Analysis* section.

Observations & Analysis

1. Describe what happened to the chalk powder mixed with mild hydrochloric acid.

   _____

   _____

   _____

2. Describe what happened to the large pieces of chalk mixed with mild hydrochloric acid.

   _____

   _____

   _____

3. Explain the chemical reaction that took place in each bowl. What kind of gas was probably produced? Why?

   _____

   _____

   _____

   _____

4. Did the amount of gas produced in the powdered sample differ from the amount of gas produced by the other sample? Explain your observations.

   _____

   _____

   _____

   _____

   _____

Lesson 50: Teacher Preparation

Basic Principle   The properties of rocks and minerals reflect the processes that formed them.

Competency   Students will construct paper models of different kinds of rock crystals.

Materials   CRYSTAL HANDOUT, scissors, glue, toothpicks

Procedure

1. Ask students if they have ever seen a precious stone such as a diamond, ruby, or emerald. Explain that such gems are three-dimensional structures called crystals made of regularly arranged atoms. Draw the arrangement of atoms in the crystal shown below. Describe the orderly arrangement of these atoms which form a neat cube of common table salt (i.e., sodium chloride). The English scientist Robert Hooke (1635–1703) was one of the first to suggest that the orderly geometric patterns seen in crystal could be used to figure out the arrangement of atoms inside the crystal. Hooke is known as the "father of crystallography," the study of crystals. The science of crystallography is crucial to the studies of minerology and chemistry.

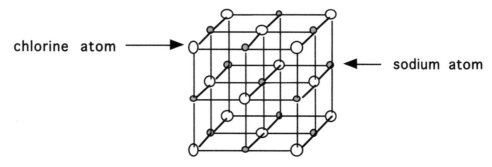

chlorine atom ⟶   ⟵ sodium atom

2. The orderly arrangement of atoms in a crystal creates surfaces, or "faces," that help us to understand how the atoms inside the crystal are arranged. Scientists classify crystals according to six basic crystalline arrangements: regular (or cubic), tetragonal, orthorhombic, hexagonal, monoclinic, and triclinic. Copy and distribute the CRYSTAL HANDOUT.

3. Assist students in completing the activity on STUDENT HANDOUT—LESSON 50.

Description of Crystalline Shapes   Students should fill out the description of each crystalline shape using the CRYSTAL HANDOUT.

Observations & Analysis

Top row from left to right: hexagonal, monoclinic, triclinic
Bottom row from left to right: regular, tetragonal, orthorhombic

Crystal Handout

REGULAR CRYSTALS have perpendicular sides of equal length.

TETRAGONAL CRYSTALS have three perpendicular sides with one long axis.

ORTHORHOMBIC CRYSTALS have three perpendicular sides with axes of different lengths.

HEXAGONAL CRYSTALS have three horizontal axes of equal lengths (at 120 degrees apart) that are perpendicular to a longer or shorter fourth axis.

MONOCLINIC CRYSTALS have three axes of different lengths with two perpendicular and one slanted axis.

TRICLINIC CRYSTALS have three axes of different lengths that meet at different angles.

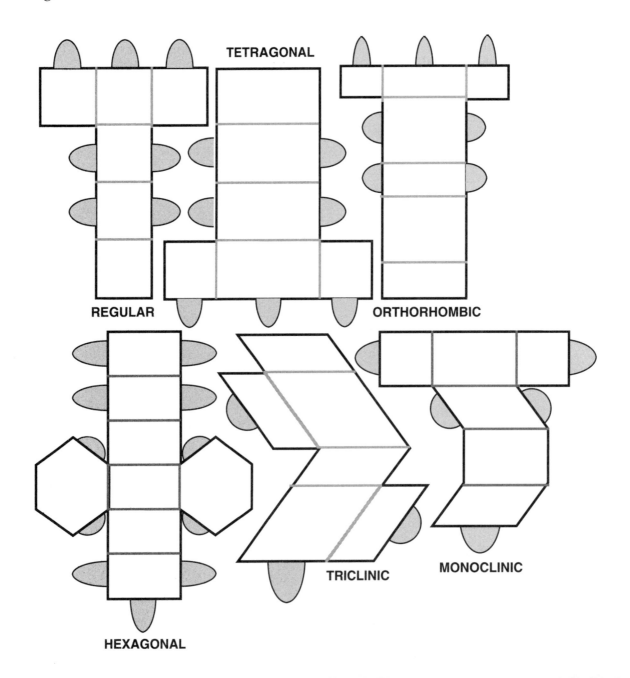

Earth Science

STUDENT HANDOUT–LESSON 50

Basic Principle   The properties of rocks and minerals reflect the processes that formed them.

Objective   Construct paper models of different kinds of crystals.

Materials   CRYSTAL HANDOUT, scissors, glue, toothpicks

Procedure

1. Write the descriptions of the different types of crystals given to you by your teacher.

2. Carefully cut out the patterns on the CRYSTAL HANDOUT.

3. Fold along the tabs and dotted lines of each pattern to form a three-dimensional structure.

4. When you are sure you have figured out the correct shape of the structure, use toothpicks to hold the tabs in place. Glue the form together.

5. Wait for the glue to dry.

6. Use a small amount of glue to fit together your shapes with the same shapes of other students. DO NOT COMBINE DIFFERENT SHAPES.

7. Use the descriptions of the different types of crystals to complete the *Observations & Analysis* section.

DESCRIPTION OF CRYSTALLINE SHAPES

regular crystals: _____

_____

tetragonal crystals:_____

_____

orthorhombic crystals:_____

_____

hexagonal crystals:_____

_____

triclinic crystals: _____

_____

monoclinic crystals: _____

_____

Observations & Analysis   Write the name of each crystalline type under the shape that most resembles it.

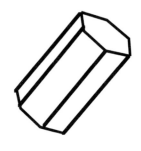

_____

_____

_____

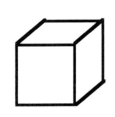

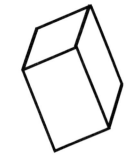

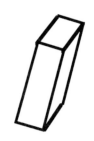

_____

_____

_____

Lesson 51: Teacher Preparation

Basic Principle The properties of rocks and minerals reflect the processes that formed them.

Competency Students will grow sodium bicarbonate crystals.

Materials water, small glasses or beakers, baking soda (sodium bicarbonate), tablespoon, paper towels, small bowl or petri dish, magnifying glass

Procedure

1. Copy and distribute the MINERAL CHARACTERISTICS CHART. Compare and contrast the characteristics of the different kinds of minerals present in rocks.
2. Assist students in completing the activity on STUDENT HANDOUT—LESSON 51.

Observations & Analysis Students' drawings will vary. They should conclude that sodium bicarbonate—like all carbonates present in minerals such as calcite— forms hexagonal crystals.

Mineral Characteristics Chart

mineral	colors	luster	acid test	crystal form	uses
quartz	colorless, pale	glassy	reacts	hexagonal	electrical equipment
calcite	colorless, white, gray, yellow, pink, blue	glassy	reacts	hexagonal	to make cement, chalk
feldspar	colorless, white, gray, pink	glassy	no reaction	monoclinic	to make porcelain
mica	pale brown, pale green, yellow	glassy, pearly	no reaction	monoclinic	electrical insulator
ice	colorless, bluish-white	glassy	no reaction	hexagonal	to lower temperature
graphite	black to gray	metallic	no reaction	hexagonal	to make "lead" pencils
silver	silver-white	metallic	reacts	regular	jewelry, coins
gold	yellow	metallic	no reaction	regular	jewelry, coins
diamond	colorless, yellow, red, blue, black	brilliant	no reaction	regular	jewelry

Earth Science

STUDENT HANDOUT–LESSON 51

Basic Principle   The properties of rocks and minerals reflect the processes that formed them.

Objective   Grow sodium bicarbonate crystals.

Materials   water, small glasses or beakers, baking soda (sodium bicarbonate), tablespoon, paper towels, small bowl or petri dish, magnifying glass

Procedure

1. Fill two small glasses or beakers halfway with water.

2. Slowly pour a tablespoon of baking soda (sodium bicarbonate) into one of the beakers and stir. Continue stirring and slowly adding baking soda to the beaker until the baking soda no longer disappears or dissolves into the solution.

3. Repeat Step 2 using the other small glass or beaker.

4. Twist a paper towel tightly into a rope.

5. Submerge one end of the towel rope into each beaker. Let the center of the towel hang over the bowl or petri dish.

6. Draw and record your observations every day at the start of class.

7. At the end of the week, examine the crystals under a magnifying glass and draw your observations.

8. Complete the *Observations & Analysis* section.

Observations & Analysis

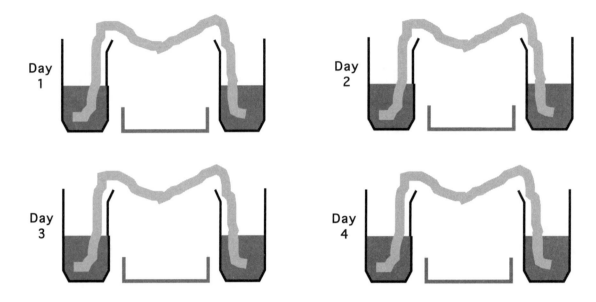

Draw your observations as seen under the magnifying glass.

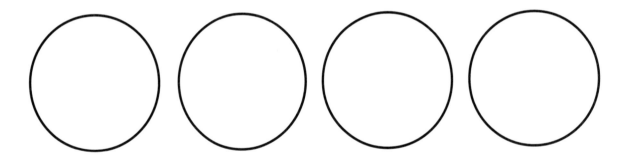

Can you identify the type of crystal formed? Explain you conclusion.

_____

_____

_____

_____

_____

Lesson 52: Teacher Preparation

Basic Principle   Identify common rock-forming minerals using a table of diagnostic properties.

Competency   Students will identify the hardness of minerals using the Mohs Scale of Hardness.

Materials   mineral samples, fingernail, penny, steel nail, cut glass

Procedure

1. Explain that minerals are classified according to their physical and chemical properties. The mineralogist examines minerals' color and luster, crystalline shape, streak and cleavage, reactivity to acids, their density relative to water (e.g., specific gravity), and their hardness. Refer to the MINERAL DIAGNOSTICS chart.

2. The German mineralogist Friedrich Mohs (1773–1839) ranked the hardness of minerals by scratching them against one another. He created a "scale of hardness" that mineralogists use to compare and identify minerals.

3. Prepare small pieces of cut glass taped at one end that students can use as part of their mineral hardness test. Assist them in completing the activity on STUDENT HANDOUT—LESSON 52. **REMIND STUDENTS TO EXERCISE CAUTION WHEN HANDLING THE CUT GLASS. THEY MUST HANDLE THE GLASS BY THE TAPE COVERING ONLY!**

Observations & Analysis

- *Answers to the questions:* Answers will vary depending upon the mineral samples provided.

- In the last question, students should summarize how they used the Mohs Scale of Hardness to begin the identification of an unknown mineral.

Mineral Diagnostics

diagnostic property	mineral determinants
color	Identify the mineral's color in the visual spectrum: red, orange, yellow, green, blue, indigo, violet.
luster	Identify the mineral's manner of reflecting light: metallic luster, nonmetallic luster, glassy, pearly, greasy, dull.
crystalline shape	Identify the mineral's crystalline shape: regular, monoclinic, triclinic, hexagonal, tetragonal, orthorhombic.
streak	Identify the color of the powdered mineral by rubbing it on a hard, white porcelain plate: colors of the visual spectrum or no color at all.
cleavage	Identify how the mineral splits with a hammer to determine the way it fractures: The mineral may cleave in thick or thin sheets, or in one or more directions.
reactivity to acids	Identify the mineral's reactivity to a number of acids (e.g., hydrochloric acid).
specific gravity	Identify the density of the mineral relative to water, which has a density equal to 1 gram per cubic centimeter.
hardness	Identify the mineral's hardness using the Mohs Scale of Hardness.

Name _____ **Date** _____

Earth Science
STUDENT HANDOUT–LESSON 52

Basic Principle   Identify common rock-forming minerals using a table of diagnostic properties.

Objective   Identify the hardness of minerals using the Mohs Scale of Hardness.

Materials   mineral samples, fingernail, penny, steel nail, cut glass

Procedure

1. Scratch the first mineral sample with the fingernail, penny, steel nail, and cut glass. **USE CAUTION WHEN HANDLING THE CUT GLASS. HANDLE THE GLASS BY THE TAPE COVERING ONLY!**

2. Record your results on the table in the *Observations & Analysis* section.

3. Repeat Steps 1 and 2 with the other mineral samples.

4. Assign each mineral a number according to the Mohs Scale of Hardness.

5. Complete the *Observations & Analysis* section.

Observations & Analysis

THE MOHS SCALE OF HARDNESS

1	2	3	4	5	6	7	8	9	10
talc	gypsum	calcite	fluorite	apatite	feldspar	quartz	topaz	corundum	diamond

fingernail 2.5   penny 3.5   steel nail 4.5   cut glass 5.5

	Mineral is softer than . . .				
mineral	fingernail	penny	steel nail	cut glass	mineral hardness

Which of the mineral samples was softer than your fingernail?_____

_____

Which of the mineral samples was softer than the penny but harder than your fingernail? _____

Which of the mineral samples was softer than the steel nail but harder than the penny? _____

Which of the mineral samples was softer than the cut glass but harder than the steel nail? _____

Were there any mineral samples harder than the cut glass? List them. _____

_____

Explain how you would use the Mohs Scale of Hardness to begin the identification of an unknown mineral.

_____

_____

 **Earth Science**

Lesson 53: Teacher Preparation

Basic Principle   The properties of rocks and minerals reflect the processes that formed them.

Competency   Students will show how the formation of cave stalagmites and stalactites occurs.

Materials   Epsom salt (magnesium sulfate), 2 small glasses or beakers, scissors, 2 small metal nuts, tablespoon, small bowl or petri dish, paper towel, cotton string

Procedure

1. Draw the diagram to help explain how stalactites and stalagmites form in a cavern. Explain that cave stalactites form when water drips through the roof of a cave and evaporates. The evaporation leaves behind deposits of calcite hanging from the roof. Stalagmites form when water drips to the floor and evaporates. The evaporation leaves behind calcite deposits which pile up on the floor of the cave.

2. Assist students in completing the activity on STUDENT HANDOUT—LESSON 53.

Observations & Analysis

- *Answer to question 2:* Epsom salts form orthorhombic crystals.
- *Answer to question 3:* Students should describe how water drips from the cavern ceiling to the floor. As it evaporates, deposits of calcite are left to form the stalactites and stalagmites.

FORMATION OF STALACTITES AND STALAGMITES

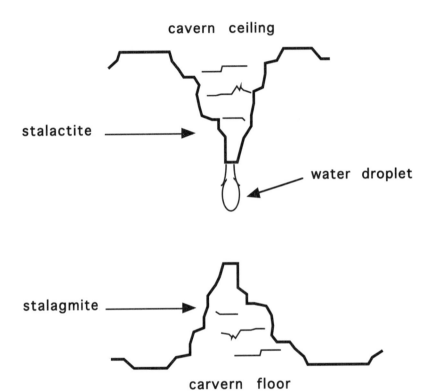

Name _____ **Date** _____

Earth Science

STUDENT HANDOUT–LESSON 53

Basic Principle   The properties of rocks and minerals reflect the processes that formed them.

Objective   Show how the formation of cave stalagmites and stalactites occurs.

Materials   Epsom salt (magnesium sulfate), 2 small glasses or beakers, scissors, 2 small metal nuts, tablespoon, small bowl or petri dish, paper towel, cotton string

Procedure

1. Pour two full tablespoons of Epsom salt into each glass or beaker.
2. Add water to the top of the Epsom salt.
3. Gently stir the mixture.
4. Cut a piece of cotton string about two feet long.
5. Tie a small metal nut to each end of the string.
6. Place the nuts tied to the string into the glasses.
7. Line the bottom of a small bowl or petri dish with paper towel.
8. Place the towel-lined bowl between the glasses.
9. Place the glasses so that the center of the string hangs about one inch above the paper towel in the bowl.
10. Let the glasses stand undisturbed for a week, out of the draft, in a moist place.
11. Complete the *Observations & Analysis* section.

Observations & Analysis

1. Draw your observations of the Epsom salt deposits.

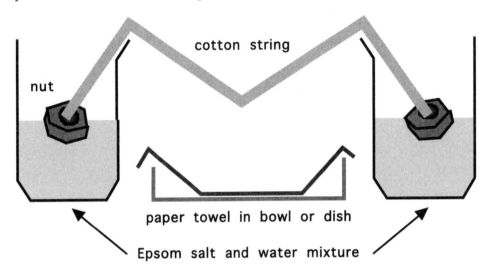

2. Can you identify the type of crystal formed? Explain your conclusion.

_____

_____

_____

3. Compare your picture of the Epsom deposits to the picture of cave stalactites and stalagmites shown. How do you think the cave deposits in the picture were formed?

_____

_____

_____

_____

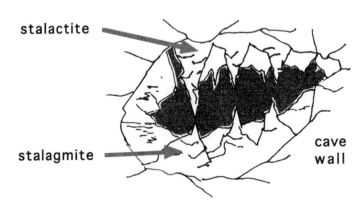

 **Earth Science**

Lesson 54: Teacher Preparation

Basic Principle   Wind can reshape the Earth's land surface.

Competency   Students will demonstrate how wind changes sand formations in deserts and beaches.

Materials   protective goggles, fine dry sand, aluminum baking tray, straws, books

Procedure

1. Draw the diagram to help students see the variety of ways that Earth's landforms are shaped and reshaped by erosion and weathering. Point out that the forces of erosion are gravity, wind, water, and glaciers. These forces cause sand and rocks to come into contact with one another resulting in abrasion and deflation. *Abrasion* is the weathering of rocks by physical contact that tends to round out the surface of rocks. *Deflation* is the removal of rocks and soil from one area to another. Explain that *weathering* is the breaking down of rocks to form soil by mechanical or chemical action.

2. Point out that desert and beach sand forms dunes that are constantly changing shape. Draw the diagram to help explain how the wind blows against the face of a dune, called the windward side, moving the sand grain up the slope and over the crest of the dune to the leeward side. The leeward side facing away from the wind is usually steeper than the windward side. The shape of the dunes depends upon the strength and direction of the wind. Dunes can move as much as a meter a day.

3. Assist students in completing the activity on STUDENT HANDOUT—LESSON 54. **MAKE SURE THEY WEAR GOGGLES TO PREVENT FINE SAND FROM GETTING INTO THEIR EYES DURING THE ACTIVITY.**

Observations & Analysis   *Answers to the questions:* Answers will vary depending upon the strength and direction of the "wind" created by the students.

FORCES THAT CHANGE THE EARTH'S LANDFORMS

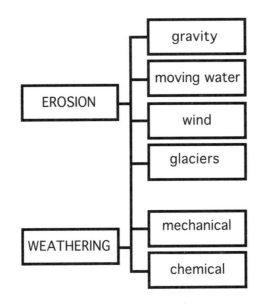

CHANGING THE SHAPE AND POSITION OF SAND DUNES

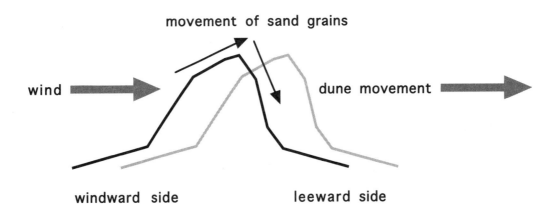

Name _____ **Date** _____

Earth Science

STUDENT HANDOUT–LESSON 54

Basic Principle   Wind can reshape the Earth's land surface.

Objective   Demonstrate how wind changes sand formations in deserts and beaches.

Materials   protective goggles, fine dry sand, aluminum baking tray, straws, books

Procedure

1. Fill the aluminum baking tray halfway with sand.

2. Set the tray at a tilt on several books.

3. Put on your goggles to prevent sand from getting into your eyes.

4. Find out how much force you need to move the sand grains around the tray. Use soft and strong "breezes" to test the wind's effects. Shift your position to study the way in which the sand rolls up into small dunes that travel in the direction of the "wind" you create.

5. Complete the _Observations & Analysis_ section.

Observations & Analysis   Record the direction and strength of the "breeze" you created. Then draw the results of your "wind" tests.

Test #1: _____

Test #2: _____

Test #3: _____

Test #4: _____

```
┌─────────────────────────┐   ┌─────────────────────────┐
│ Test #1                 │   │ Test #2                 │
│                         │   │                         │
│                         │   │                         │
│                         │   │                         │
│                         │   │                         │
└─────────────────────────┘   └─────────────────────────┘
┌─────────────────────────┐   ┌─────────────────────────┐
│ Test #3                 │   │ Test #4                 │
│                         │   │                         │
│                         │   │                         │
│                         │   │                         │
│                         │   │                         │
└─────────────────────────┘   └─────────────────────────┘
```

Compare your drawings to the dune patterns created in desert and beach sand. Were you able to create any of the patterns shown below?

barchan
formed in limited sand during strong, constant wind

transverse
formed in plentiful sand during strong wind in one direction

star
formed in plentiful sand during strong, shifting wind

linear
formed along seacoasts where sea and land breezes mix

parabolic
formed along seacoasts where plants hold the sand in place

_____

_____

_____

_____

Lesson 55: Teacher Preparation

Basic Principle   Water can reshape the Earth's land surface.

Competency   Students will demonstrate how water changes sand and soil formations.

Materials   protective goggles, fine dry sand, potting soil, pebbles, 3 aluminum baking trays, large pitcher, water, books

Procedure

1. Review the variety of ways that Earth's landforms are shaped and reshaped by erosion and weathering using the diagram in Teacher Preparation of LESSON 54. Point out that the degree of water erosion produced in a landform depends upon the rate of water flow as well as the characteristics of the rocks and soils covering the landform. Draw the pictures given here to show how water flow over long periods of time can transform a river.

2. Assist students in completing the activity on STUDENT HANDOUT—LESSON 55. **MAKE SURE THEY WEAR GOGGLES TO PREVENT SAND AND SOIL FROM GETTING INTO THEIR EYES DURING THE ACTIVITY.**

Observations & Analysis

- *Answer to the tests:* Test results will vary depending upon the rate of water flow and the characteristics of the rocks and soils used in the test.

- *Answer to the question:* Students should conclude that the flow of water has accumulative effects that result in the formation of winding rivers and deep canyons such as the Grand Canyon.

LIFE OF A RIVER

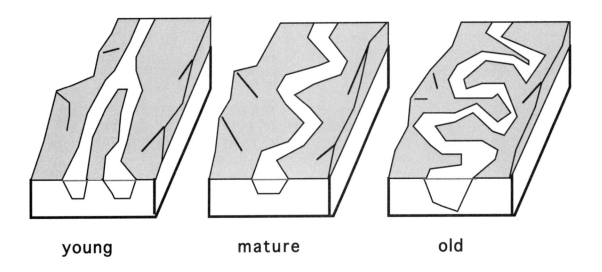

young   mature   old

Name _____ **Date** _____

Earth Science
STUDENT HANDOUT–LESSON 55

Basic Principle   Water can reshape the Earth's land surface.

Objective   Demonstrate how water changes sand and soil formations.

Materials   protective goggles, fine dry sand, potting soil, pebbles, 3 aluminum baking trays, large pitcher, water, books

Procedure

1. Fill one aluminum baking tray halfway with fine sand.
2. Fill one aluminum baking tray halfway with fine sand and pebbles.
3. Fill the other aluminum baking tray halfway with potting soil.
4. Set the trays at a tilt on several books.
5. Put on your goggles to prevent splattering sand or soil from getting into your eyes.
6. Fill the large pitcher with water.
7. Pour the water over the surface of the sand and soil to test the effects of water flow on the land's surface. Vary the tilt of the trays to control the speed of the water. Test different amounts of water flowing at different speeds as suggested in the *Observations & Analysis* section.
8. Complete the *Observations & Analysis* section.

Set tray on books to control speed of water flow.

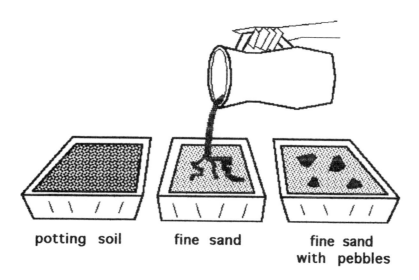

potting soil   fine sand   fine sand
with pebbles

Observations & Analysis   Draw the results of each test.

POTTING-SOIL TESTS

A **small** amount of **slowly** flowing water

A **small** amount of **quickly** flowing water

A **large** amount of **slowly** flowing water

A **large** amount of **quickly** flowing water

FINE-SAND TESTS

A **small** amount of **slowly** flowing water

A **small** amount of **quickly** flowing water

A **large** amount of **slowly** flowing water

A **large** amount of **quickly** flowing water

FINE-SAND-WITH-PEBBLES TESTS

A **small** amount of **slowly** flowing water

A **small** amount of **quickly** flowing water

A **large** amount of **slowly** flowing water

A **large** amount of **quickly** flowing water

Predict how the surface of the land would change if a slowly flowing stream were allowed to flow for millions of years.

_____

_____

_____

_____

Lesson 56: Teacher Preparation

Basic Principle   Natural processes, including freezing and thawing, cause rocks to break.

Competency   Students will show that water expands when freezing.

Materials   2 straws, modeling clay, water, freezer, tape, marking pen, paper towels

Procedure

1. Review the variety of ways that Earth's landforms are shaped and reshaped by erosion and weathering using the diagram in Teacher Preparation of LESSON 54. Point out that the degree of weathering produced in a landform depends upon the severity of temperature variations and the characteristics of the rocks and soils covering the landform. Draw a picture like the one shown here to show how freezing water cracks rock formations.

2. Assist students in completing the activity on STUDENT HANDOUT—LESSON 56.

Observations & Analysis

- Students' drawings and descriptions should reflect the observation that water expands as it freezes, causing the clay stoppers to "pop out" of the ends of the straw.

- *Answer to the question:* Students should conclude that water expands as it freezes, a process that can result in the breaking of rocks, soil, and even sidewalk cement.

ICE-CRACKED ROCK FORMATIONS

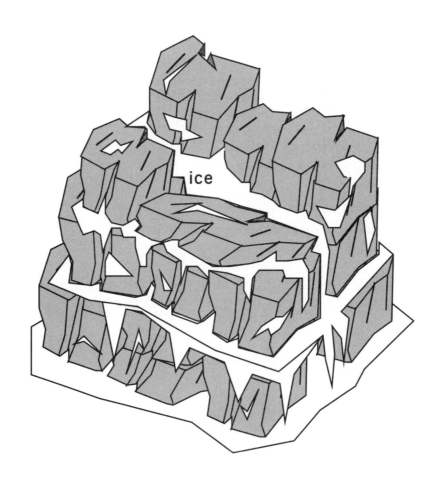

Name _____ **Date** _____

Earth Science

STUDENT HANDOUT–LESSON 56

Basic Principle   Natural processes, including freezing and thawing, cause rocks to break.

Objective   Show that water expands when freezing.

Materials   2 straws, modeling clay, water, freezer, tape, marking pen, paper towels

Procedure

1. Fill two plastic or paper straws with water. Plug the ends of each straw with modeling clay. Make sure there are no air bubbles left inside the straws.

2. Label one straw "A" and the other straw "B" with a piece of tape.

3. Draw the two straws side-by-side in the box marked "BEFORE" in the *Observations & Analysis* section.

4. Wrap each straw in a paper towel. Place straw "A" in the freezer compartment of a refrigerator. Place straw "B" on top of the refrigerator.

5. Examine the straws 24 hours later. Draw both straws side-by-side in the box marked "AFTER" in the *Observations & Analysis* section.

6. Complete the *Observations & Analysis* section.

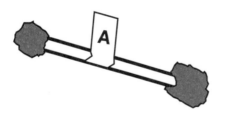 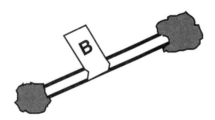

water-filled   straws

Observations & Analysis

BEFORE	AFTER

Describe what happened to each straw.

_____

_____

_____

_____

Explain your observations. Form a conclusion about what happens to water as it freezes.

_____

_____

_____

_____

_____

_____

_____

Lesson 57: Teacher Preparation

Basic Principle   Natural processes, including freezing and thawing, cause rocks to break.

Competency   Students will show that freezing water can break hard materials such as metals and rocks.

Materials   empty soda can, water, freezer

Procedure

1. Review the variety of ways that Earth's landforms are shaped and reshaped by erosion and weathering using the diagram in Teacher Preparation of LESSON 54. As in Teacher Preparation of Lessons 49 and 56, point out that the degree of weathering produced in a landform depends upon the severity of temperature variations and the characteristics of the rocks and soils covering the landform. Draw a picture like the one given here to show how advancing and receding glaciers can create deep glacial river valleys.

2. Assist students in completing the activity on STUDENT HANDOUT—LESSON 57. **WARN STUDENTS TO AVOID TOUCHING THE SHARP EDGES OF THE TORN CAN METAL.**

Observations & Analysis

• Students' drawings and descriptions should reflect the observation that water expands as it freezes, resulting in the tearing of the can metal.

• *Answer to the question:* Students should conclude that water expands as it freezes, a process that can result in the breaking of rocks and soil.

ADVANCING AND RECEDING GLACIERS CHANGE THE LAND

mountain range

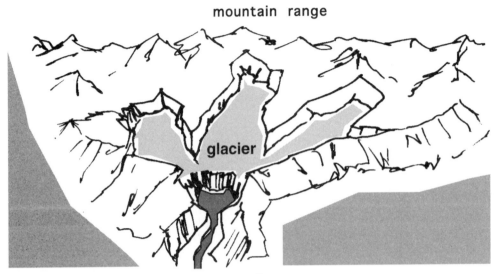

glacier river valley

AN ADVANCING GLACIER

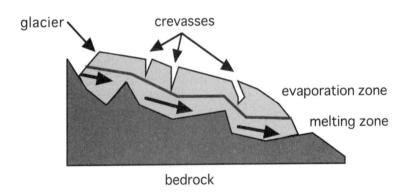

bedrock

The top of the glacier is called the **fracture zone** with **crevasses** as deep as 150 meters. Under pressure, the bottom of the glacier, called the **flow zone**, liquifies and flows downhill carrying the ice sheet with it. A glacier that moves downhill more rapidly than its lower end or "foot" melts is said to be "advancing." A glacier with a foot that melts back faster than the glacier moves downhill is said to be "receding." If the melting occurs at the same rate as the downward movement of the ice, then the glacier appears to be stationary.

Name _____ **Date** _____

Earth Science
STUDENT HANDOUT–LESSON 57

Basic Principle   Natural processes, including freezing and thawing, cause rocks to break.

Objective   Show that freezing water can break hard materials such as metals and rocks.

Materials   empty soda can, water, freezer

Procedure

1. Fill an empty soda can to the brim with water.

2. Draw the water-filled soda can in the box marked "BEFORE" in the _Observations & Analysis_ section.

3. Place the can in the freezer compartment of a refrigerator.

4. Examine the can 24 hours later. **BE CAREFUL NOT TO TOUCH THE RAGGED EDGES OF SPLIT METAL.** Draw the can in the box marked "AFTER" in the _Observations & Analysis_ section.

5. Complete the _Observations & Analysis_ section.

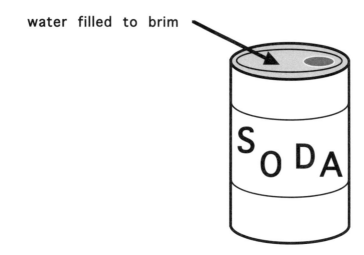

water filled to brim

Observations & Analysis

BEFORE	AFTER

Describe what happened to the can.

_____

_____

_____

_____

Explain your observations. Form a conclusion about what can happen to rocks surrounded by water as it freezes.

_____

_____

_____

_____

_____

_____

_____

Lesson 58: Teacher Preparation

Basic Principle   Some changes in the Earth are due to slow processes, such as weathering, erosion, and slow movement of Earth's crustal plates.

Competency   Students will show how the Earth's crustal plates move about on the surface of our planet.

Materials   protective goggles, pie tin, cardboard, hot plate, water, marking pen, scissors

Procedure

1. Draw the top picture to illustrate the interior of the Earth. Inform students that the thickness of Earth's crust is hardly one one-hundredth (about 1%) the distance from the Earth surface to its center. The Earth's hot molten mantle made of iron and nickel swirls in eddies and currents that crack the crust into separate "plates" that move and collide on the surface. The movement of these crustal plates has changed the continental features of our planet's surface over the eons.

2. Draw the bottom picture to illustrate the kind of features formed by the motion and collision of the plates. Point out how plates "converge" and "diverge." Refer to Teacher Preparation of LESSON 59; and, if a map of the Earth is available, point out the most prominent plates and collision zones: the larger Pacific, North American, South American, African, Eurasian, Antarctic, and Indo-Australian plates, as well as the smaller Arabian, Philippine, Nazca (west coast of South America), Cocos (west coast of Central America), and Caribbean plates. Identify major oceanic trenches in the Pacific Ocean (such as the Marianas trench off the eastern border of the Philippine plate) where plates collide—one plate being subducted back into the mantle under another. Point out that new crust is continually being created at divergent zones called rift valleys where the sea floor is spreading apart.

3. Assist students in completing the activity on STUDENT HANDOUT—LESSON 58. **MAKE SURE THEY WEAR GOGGLES TO PREVENT HOT WATER FROM SPLATTERING INTO THEIR EYES.**

Observations & Analysis

- *Answer to question 1:* The puzzle pieces move apart.
- *Answer to question 2:* The crustal plates that cover the surface of the Earth move and collide. This changes the continental features of the Earth's surface as well as land features along continental borders.
- Students' drawings will vary.

THE STRUCTURE OF THE EARTH

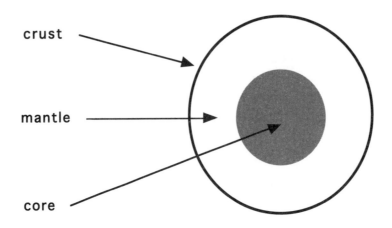

crust

mantle

core

EARTH'S PLATES IN COLLISION

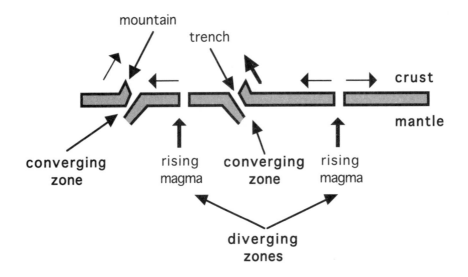

mountain

trench

crust

mantle

converging
zone

rising
magma

converging
zone

rising
magma

diverging
zones

Plates are pushed apart at diverging zones by upswelling magma from the mantle. The magma cools in the depths of the ocean to form new crust. The plates collide on the other side of the world at converging zones, forcing heavier rock to sink back into the mantle. At "hot spots" around the globe, magma can burst through the crust in the middle of a plate creating volcanic midoceanic islands like the Hawaiian Islands.

Name _____   **Date** _____

Earth Science
STUDENT HANDOUT–LESSON 58

Basic Principle   Some changes in the Earth are due to slow processes, such as weathering, erosion, and slow movement of Earth's crustal plates.

Objective   Show how the Earth's crustal plates move about on the surface of our planet.

Materials   protective goggles, pie tin, cardboard, hot plate, water, marking pen, scissors

Procedure

1. Cut a piece of thick cardboard into a circle about six inches across.
2. Use a marking pen to draw five or six puzzle pieces on the cardboard circle.
3. Use the scissors to carefully cut out the puzzle pieces.
4. Fill the pie tin halfway with water.
5. Place the water-filled pie tin on the hot plate.
6. Gently put the puzzle pieces together. Place the circle gently in the middle of the water-filled pie tin.
7. Put on your goggles to prevent hot water from splattering into your eyes.
8. Turn the hot plate on and set it to medium heat.
9. Turn off the hot plate after five minutes of heating.
10. Complete the *Observations & Analysis* section.

water-filled pie tin with reassembled puzzle

Observations & Analysis

1. Describe what happens to the puzzle pieces as the water in the pie tin gets warmer.

    _____

    _____

    _____

    _____

2. Explain your observations. Form a conclusion about what happens to the crustal plates of the Earth floating on molten hot magma.

    _____

    _____

    _____

    _____

    _____

    _____

3. Draw a picture of the position of your puzzle pieces at the start of the experiment and after five minutes of heating.

AT THE START	AFTER FIVE MINUTES

 **Earth Science**

Lesson 59: Teacher Preparation

Basic Principle   Some changes in the Earth are due to slow processes, such as weathering, erosion, and slow movement of Earth's crustal plates.

Competency   Students will show how the Earth's crustal plates press together to form mountain ranges and folds.

Materials   3 colors of modeling clay, butter knife

Procedure

1. Copy and distribute the map to illustrate the Earth's major crustal plates. Shaded arrows indicate the general direction in which the plates are presently moving. The longest diverging zone is the Mid-Atlantic Ridge located in the middle of the Atlantic Ocean. Major converging zones are found in the eastern Pacific Ocean along the Japanese and Philippine Islands.

2. The theory that explains how the Earth's crustal plates move is called the "theory of plate tectonics" or the "theory of continental drift." It was first proposed by German geophysicist Alfred Lothar Wegener (1880–1930). Geologists can measure the rate at which the continental plates are moving. On average, the continents travel several inches (≈ 2–4 centimeters) every year. But given millions of years they will move a considerable distance. The theory of plate tectonics is supported by several pieces of evidence: (1) the movement of the plates can be measured, (2) the edges of distant continents resemble puzzle pieces that can be assembled into a large "mother continent," (3) identical plant and animal fossils found on distant continents are the remains of organisms that must have evolved in exactly the same place, and (4) the Earth's major earthquake zones are located in regions of maximum earthquake activity that mark out the edges of the continental plates.

3. Assist students in completing the activity on STUDENT HANDOUT—LESSON 59.

Observations & Analysis   *Answer to the questions:* Students' drawings and observations will vary. However, students should be able to compare their creations to the kinds of folds and faults shown in the illustrations on STUDENT HANDOUT—LESSON 59.

Earth's Major Crustal Plates

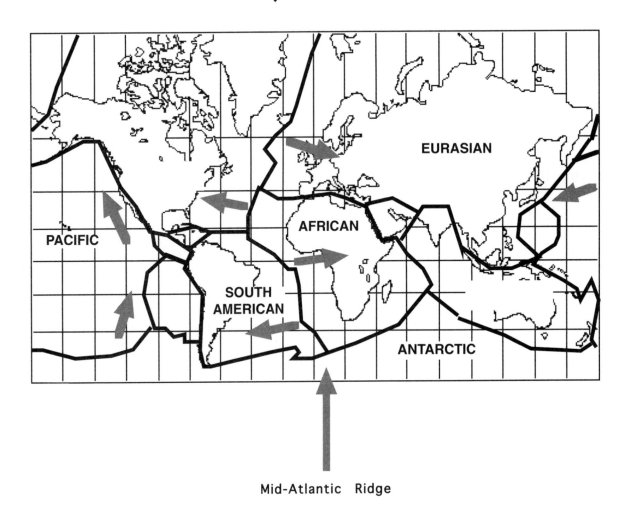

Mid-Atlantic Ridge

Earth Science
STUDENT HANDOUT–LESSON 59

Basic Principle   Some changes in the Earth are due to slow processes, such as weathering, erosion, and slow movement of Earth's crustal plates.

Objective   Show how the Earth's crustal plates press together to form mountain ranges and folds.

Materials   3 colors of modeling clay, butter knife

Procedure

1. Use each color of modeling clay to make seven flat, clay squares about three inches wide.

2. Make seven three-layer blocks using three different colors for each block. Press the three layers together tightly.

3. Compress the first block slowly from the sides. This will show how the "compression" of a single crustal plate produces folds in the Earth's crustal layers. Draw your result in the box titled "FOLDED PLATE."

4. "Collide" the other plates together in pairs at varying speeds and angles to see if you can produce the other types of mountain features shown in the *Observations & Analysis* section. Draw the formations you create.

5. Complete the *Observations & Analysis* section.

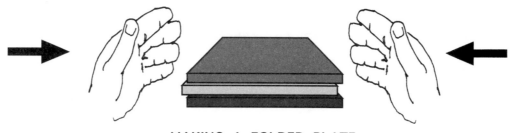

MAKING A FOLDED PLATE

Observations & Analysis Describe what happened in each "folding" or "collision" trial. Don't forget to record how quickly (slow or fast) you pressed the two plates together. Then draw your observations.

folding trial: _____

collision trial #1: _____

collision trial #2: _____

collision trial #3: _____

FOLDED PLATE	COLLISION TRIAL #1

COLLISION TRIAL #2	COLLISION TRIAL #3

Compare your drawings with the collision patterns created along plate boundaries (or fault lines) around the world. Were you able to create any of the patterns shown below?

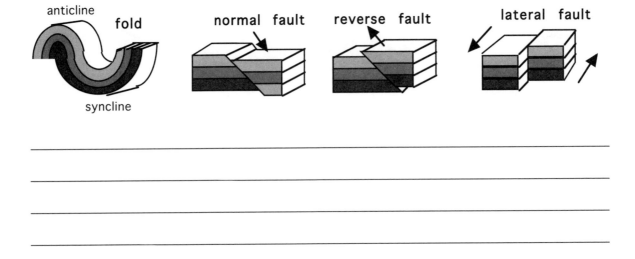

anticline   **fold**   **normal fault**   **reverse fault**   **lateral fault**

syncline

_____

_____

_____

_____

 **Earth Science**

Lesson 60: Teacher Preparation

Basic Principle   Some changes in the Earth are due to rapid processes, such as landslides, volcanic eruptions, and earthquakes.

Competency   Students will show how the pressure builds up in volcanoes, resulting in their periodic eruptions.

Materials   protective goggles, large beaker, glass funnel, hot plate

Procedure

1. Review the forces that cause the Earth's crustal plates to move. Remind students that currents in the molten magma of the mantle push the plates apart or into collision. Any place where molten magma rises to the Earth's surface is called a "vent." Volcanoes form where magma cools and hardens on the surface. Most of our planet's volcanoes are located under the ocean at mid-ocean ridges. Others are found at places where the plates collide. Some, like the Hawaiian Islands, are found in the middle of a plate over a portion of mantle called a "hot spot." Draw the illustration of the four main Hawaiian Islands to show how hot spots in the Earth's mantle formed the islands as the Pacific plate twisted over the hot spot in the past four million years. Volcanoes erupt when the pressure caused by magma and expanding gases inside the volcano becomes greater than the strength of the volcano's hardened walls.

2. Point out that "geysers" form in areas that are volcanically active. A geyser is a hot spring where water over a vent is heated to extreme temperatures and turned into steam. The steam is forced out of the cracks in the Earth where it gushes up in dramatic bursts. The country of Iceland has about 30 active geysers because it lies along the path of the Mid-Atlantic Ridge. Yellowstone National Park in Wyoming, a volcanically active region that last erupted about 600,000 years ago, is noted for more than 200 geysers. The park is located where the Pacific and North American plates slide past one another.

3. Assist students in completing the activity on STUDENT HANDOUT—LESSON 60. **WARN THEM TO WEAR GOGGLES TO PREVENT HOT WATER FROM SPLATTERING INTO THEIR EYES.**

Observations & Analysis

- *Answer to question 2:* During the timing period, the water will heat up and begin to bubble until the water erupts in periodic bursts.

- *Answer to question 3:* Students should explain how the molten lava that erupts from volcanoes eventually cools and hardens. Later eruptions add to the cooled landforms until an entire volcano is built.

FORMATION OF THE HAWAIIAN ISLANDS

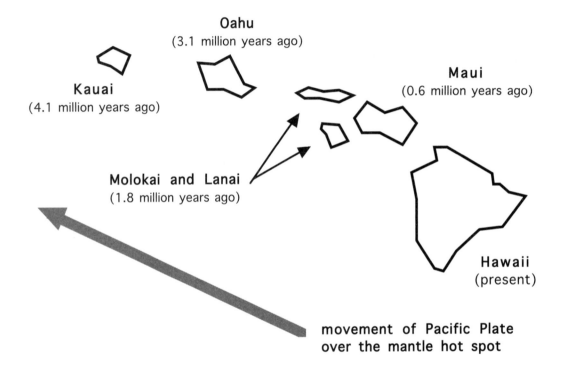

Oahu
(3.1 million years ago)

Kauai
(4.1 million years ago)

Maui
(0.6 million years ago)

Molokai and Lanai
(1.8 million years ago)

Hawaii
(present)

movement of Pacific Plate
over the mantle hot spot

Name _____ Date _____

Earth Science

STUDENT HANDOUT–LESSON 60

Basic Principle   Some changes in the Earth are due to rapid processes, such as landslides, volcanic eruptions, and earthquakes.

Objective   Show how the pressure builds up in volcanoes, resulting in their periodic eruptions.

Materials   protective goggles, large beaker, glass funnel, hot plate

Procedure

1. Fill the large beaker about one-quarter full with water.
2. Invert the glass funnel into the water as shown.
3. Put on your protective goggles to prevent hot water from splattering into your eyes.
4. Turn on the hot plate to a medium setting.
5. Record your observations every minute for ten minutes.
6. Complete the *Observations & Analysis* section.

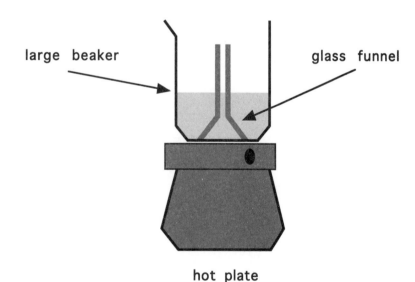

large beaker   glass funnel

hot plate

Observations & Analysis

1. Describe what happens every minute for ten minutes.

   After 1 minute: _____

   After 2 minutes: _____

   After 3 minutes: _____

   After 4 minutes: _____

   After 5 minutes: _____

   After 6 minutes: _____

   After 7 minutes: _____

   After 8 minutes: _____

   After 9 minutes: _____

   After 10 minutes: _____

2. Did the water eruption occur in a continuous flow or did it erupt in bursts?
   Explain your answer.

   _____

   _____

   _____

3. Use the diagram shown below to explain how volcanoes are built.

   _____

   _____

   _____

   _____

   _____

   _____

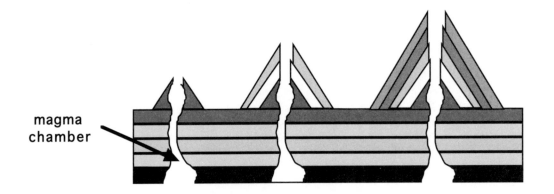

magma
chamber

 **Earth Science**

Lesson 61: Teacher Preparation

Basic Principle   Some changes in the Earth are due to slow processes, such as weathering, erosion, and slow movement of Earth's crustal plates.

Competency   Students will show how landforms are eroded by abrasion.

Materials   2 grades of sandpaper (fine and rough), a block of soft balsa wood, a block of hard pine wood, magnifying glass

Procedure

1. Review the variety of ways that Earth's landforms are shaped and reshaped by erosion and weathering using the diagram in Teacher Preparation of LESSON 54. Point out that the degree of wind and water erosion produced in a landform depends upon the rate of wind and water flow as well as the characteristics of the rocks and soils covering the landform.

2. Define the term "abrasion" as weathering by physical contact. Abrasion produced by small particles carried by the wind or in water results in the rounding of rocks.

3. Assist students in completing the activity on STUDENT HANDOUT—LESSON 61.

Observations & Analysis

- *Answer to the tests:* Students should observe that rubbing the soft balsa wood with rough sandpaper produced the widest and deepest scoring marks. Rubbing fine sandpaper on harder pine produces less scoring.

- *Answer to question 3:* Students should conclude that hard rock will weather more slowly than soft rock.

- *Answer to question 4:* Students should explain that formations such as those shown in the drawing are formed by wind abrasion. The different hardnesses of the layers of sediment in the rocks give rise to the odd shapes that cover the land-form.

WEATHERING BY ABRASION

hard sedimentary layers
sustain less weathering

soft sedimentary layers
sustain greater weathering

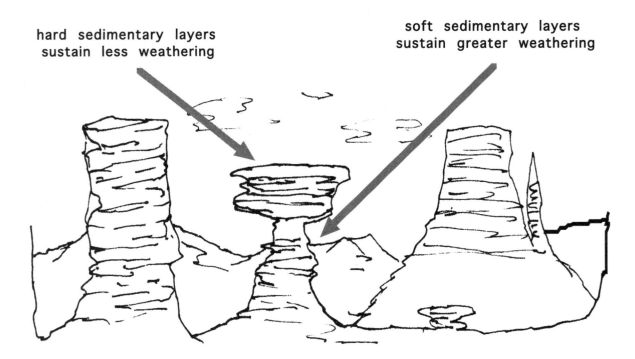

Earth Science
STUDENT HANDOUT–LESSON 61

Basic Principle Some changes in the Earth are due to slow processes, such as weathering, erosion, and slow movement of Earth's crustal plates.

Objective Show how landforms are eroded by abrasion.

Materials 2 grades of sandpaper (fine and rough), a block of soft balsa wood, a block of hard pine wood, magnifying glass

Procedure

1. Rub one side of each block of wood with fine-grade sandpaper.

2. Rub another side of each block of wood with rough-grade sandpaper.

3. Complete the *Observations & Analysis* section.

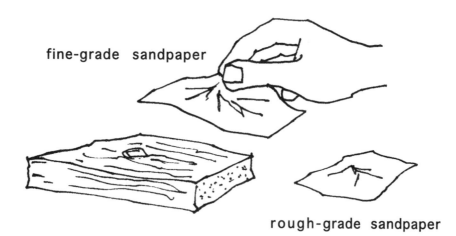

fine-grade sandpaper

rough-grade sandpaper

Observations & Analysis

1. Define *abrasion*: _____

   _____

2. Examine the sides of each block of wood. Describe the scratch patterns made by each grade of sandpaper. Give special attention to the width and depth of the scratches.

   soft wood/fine sandpaper: _____

   _____

   soft wood/rough sandpaper: _____

   _____

   hard wood/fine sandpaper: _____

   _____

   hard wood/rough sandpaper: _____

   _____

3. Explain your observations. What kinds of rock would be eroded more quickly than others by wind or water abrasion?

   _____

   _____

   _____

4. Explain how the rock formations shown below were probably formed.

   _____

   _____

   _____

Lesson 62: Teacher Preparation

Basic Principle   Some changes in the Earth are due to slow processes, such as weathering, erosion, and slow movement of Earth's crustal plates.

Competency   Students will show how different kinds of soil affect the flow of water through Earth landforms.

Materials   fine sand, potting soil, gravel or pebbles, 3 coffee filters, funnel, 2 glass jars or beakers, water, stopwatch or wristwatch with second hand

Procedure

1. Review the variety of ways that Earth's landforms are shaped and reshaped by erosion and weathering using the diagram in Teacher Preparation of LESSON 54. Point out that different kinds of soil permit the flow of water at different rates.

2. Define the term "porosity" as the amount of air space in the soil compared to the total volume of the soil. The greater the number and size of the air spaces, the more easily water flows through the soil.

3. Define the term "percolation" as the gradual draining or oozing of water through "porous" rocks or soil. More porous rock permits greater amounts of percolation.

4. Assist students in completing the activity on STUDENT HANDOUT—LESSON 62.

Observations & Analysis

- *Answer to the tests:* Students should observe that gravel or pebbles permit the water to flow in the least amount of time. The degree of flow measured in the fine sand and potting soil tests will depend upon the particular characteristics of the type of sand and soil used.

- *Answer to question 3:* Students should conclude that more porous rocks and soil allow for greater degrees of weathering by water abrasion.

Earth Science

STUDENT HANDOUT–LESSON 62

Basic Principle   Some changes in the Earth are due to slow processes, such as weathering, erosion, and slow movement of Earth's crustal plates.

Objective   Show how different kinds of soil affect the flow of water through Earth landforms.

Materials   fine sand, potting soil, gravel or pebbles, 3 coffee filters, funnel, 2 glass jars or beakers, water, stopwatch or wristwatch with second hand

Procedure

1. Line the funnel with one of the coffee filters. Place the funnel into one of the glass jars (or beakers).

2. Fill the filter with fine sand.

3. Fill one of the glass jars or beakers with water.

4. Slowly pour the water into the sand-filled funnel. Use the stopwatch or wristwatch second hand to time how long it takes for the water to run completely through the sand.

5. Record the result in the *Observations & Analysis* section.

6. Repeat Steps 1 through 5 using a new coffee filter for the potting soil and then the gravel (or pebble) samples.

7. Complete the *Observations & Analysis* section.

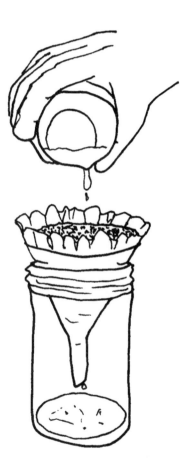

Observations & Analysis

1. Define these terms.

   porosity: _____

   _____

   percolation: _____

   _____

2. The tests.

   Time for water to percolate through the fine sand: _____

   Time for water to percolate through the potting soil: _____

   Time for water to percolate through the gravel (or pebbles): _____

3. Explain how the porosity of the soil might affect the way a landform erodes.

   _____

   _____

   _____

   _____

   _____

   _____

   _____

   _____

   _____

   _____

   _____

FOURTH-GRADE LEVEL

Earth Science

PRACTICE TEST

Earth Science

PRACTICE TEST

Directions: Use the diagram of THE ROCK CYCLE shown below to answer questions 1 through 5. (Use the Answer Sheet.)

THE ROCK CYCLE

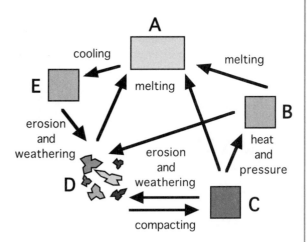

1. Which letter shows magma?

2. Which letter shows sedimentary rock?

3. Which letter shows igneous rock?

4. Which letter shows metamorphic rock?

5. Which letter shows sediment?

Directions: Use the Answer Sheet to darken the letter of the phrase that best answers each question.

6. Which of the following would best help to identify a rock that once contained seashells?

   (A) Mohs Scale of Hardness

   (B) a spring balance

   (C) an acid test

   (D) a magnifying glass

   (E) a measure of density

7. Which of the following affects how quickly a rock breaks apart?

   (A) the rock's composition

   (B) the rock's surface area

   (C) the rock's location

   (D) temperature

   (E) all of the above

8. How are crystals formed?

   (A) mixing of sediment

   (B) hardening of clay

   (C) weathering of soil

   (D) abrasion of stone

   (E) cooling of molten rock

9. Which of the following can be determined by examining the crystals in a rock?

   (A) the rock's weight

   (B) the minerals present in the rock

   (C) the age of the rock

   (D) the rock's density

   (E) none of the above

Directions: Use Mohs Scale of Hardness to answer questions 10 through 14. (Use the Answer Sheet.)

MOHS SCALE OF HARDNESS

1	talc
2	gypsum
3	calcite
4	fluorite
5	apatite
6	feldspar
7	quartz
8	topaz
9	corundum
10	diamond

---

10. Which of the following is the hardest mineral on the Mohs scale?

    (A) gypsum

    (B) fluorite

    (C) feldspar

    (D) topaz

    (E) diamond

11. Which of the following would scratch a piece of quartz?

    (A) talc

    (B) feldspar

    (C) fluorite

    (D) topaz

    (E) calcite

12. What is the hardness of a mineral that can scratch calcite but not fluorite?

    (A) 3

    (B) between 3 and 4

    (C) 4

    (D) between 4 and 5

    (E) 5

13. John used a piece of cut glass to scratch a piece of apatite. The cut glass was not able to scratch a piece of feldspar. What is the hardness of the cut glass?

    (A) 3.5

    (B) 4

    (C) 4.5

    (D) 5

    (E) 5.5

14. A steel nail will scratch a piece of gypsum but not a piece of corundum. What is the hardness of a steel nail?

    (A) between 1 and 2

    (B) between 3 and 4

    (C) between 6 and 7

    (D) between 9 and 10

    (E) More tests are needed to find the hardness of the nail.

Directions: Use the drawing of the cave shown below to answer questions 15 through 17. (Use the Answer Sheet.)

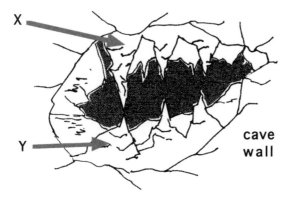

15. Which of the following best describes formation "X"?

    (A) icicle

    (B) lava

    (C) runoff

    (D) stalactite

    (E) stalagmite

16. Which of the following best describes formation "Y"?

    (A) icicle

    (B) lava

    (C) runoff

    (D) stalactite

    (E) stalagmite

17. Which of the following best describes how formations "X" and "Y" were made?

    (A) abrasion

    (B) deflation

    (C) percolation

    (D) melting

    (E) freezing

Directions: Use the drawing of the rock formation shown below to answer questions 18 and 19. (Use the Answer Sheet.)

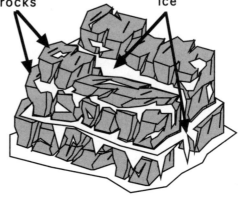

18. Which of the following terms best describes how the cracks formed in the rocks?

    (A) abrasion

    (B) deflation

    (C) percolation

    (D) weathering

    (E) erosion

19. What physical process most likely caused the rocks to crack?

    (A) water flowing

    (B) water freezing

    (C) water evaporating

    (D) water boiling

    (E) none of the above

20. Which of the following best describes the formation of sand dunes?

    (A) abrasion

    (B) deflation

    (C) percolation

    (D) weathering

    (E) waving

21. Which of the following terms best describes how the desert sculptures shown below were formed?

(A) abrasion

(B) inflation

(C) perspiration

(D) glaciation

(E) invention

Directions: The diagram below shows one volcano at three different periods in its lifetime. The volcano has erupted on schedule every 10,000 years since its first eruption. The most recent eruption occurred last year. Use the diagram to answer questions 22 and 23. (Use the Answer Sheet.)

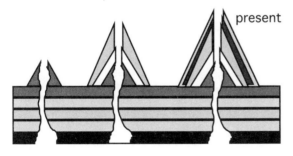

present

22. When did the volcano first erupt?

(A) 10,000 years ago

(B) 20,000 years ago

(C) 30,000 years ago

(D) 40,000 years ago

(E) 50,000 years ago

23. When did the volcano's most violent eruption probably occur?

(A) 10,000 years ago

(B) 20,000 years ago

(C) 30,000 years ago

(D) 40,000 years ago

(E) 50,000 years ago

24. The diagram below shows five volcanic islands on a crustal plate. The plate is moving west. Which volcanic island is the oldest?

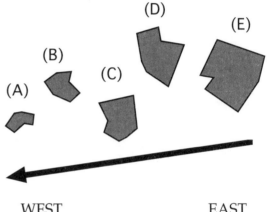

WEST   EAST

25. Which of the following causes earthquakes?

(A) tornadoes

(B) hurricanes

(C) the movement of the Earth's crust

(D) sun spots

(E) eclipses

Earth Science

PRACTICE TEST: ANSWER SHEET

Name _____ **Date** _____ **Period** _____

Darken the circle above the letter that best answers the question.

	A	B	C	D	E		A	B	C	D	E
1.	○	○	○	○	○	14.	○	○	○	○	○
2.	○	○	○	○	○	15.	○	○	○	○	○
3.	○	○	○	○	○	16.	○	○	○	○	○
4.	○	○	○	○	○	17.	○	○	○	○	○
5.	○	○	○	○	○	18.	○	○	○	○	○
6.	○	○	○	○	○	19.	○	○	○	○	○
7.	○	○	○	○	○	20.	○	○	○	○	○
8.	○	○	○	○	○	21.	○	○	○	○	○
9.	○	○	○	○	○	22.	○	○	○	○	○
10.	○	○	○	○	○	23.	○	○	○	○	○
11.	○	○	○	○	○	24.	○	○	○	○	○
12.	○	○	○	○	○	25.	○	○	○	○	○
13.	○	○	○	○	○						

Earth Science

KEY TO PRACTICE TEST

1. ● A   ○ B   ○ C   ○ D   ○ E
2. ○ A   ○ B   ● C   ○ D   ○ E
3. ○ A   ○ B   ○ C   ○ D   ● E
4. ○ A   ● B   ○ C   ○ D   ○ E
5. ○ A   ○ B   ○ C   ● D   ○ E
6. ○ A   ○ B   ● C   ○ D   ○ E
7. ○ A   ○ B   ○ C   ○ D   ● E
8. ○ A   ○ B   ○ C   ○ D   ● E
9. ○ A   ● B   ○ C   ○ D   ○ E
10. ○ A   ○ B   ○ C   ○ D   ● E
11. ○ A   ○ B   ○ C   ● D   ○ E
12. ○ A   ● B   ○ C   ○ D   ○ E
13. ○ A   ○ B   ○ C   ○ D   ● E

14. ○ A   ○ B   ○ C   ○ D   ● E
15. ○ A   ○ B   ○ C   ● D   ○ E
16. ○ A   ○ B   ○ C   ○ D   ● E
17. ○ A   ○ B   ● C   ○ D   ○ E
18. ○ A   ○ B   ○ C   ● D   ○ E
19. ○ A   ● B   ○ C   ○ D   ○ E
20. ○ A   ● B   ○ C   ○ D   ○ E
21. ● A   ○ B   ○ C   ○ D   ○ E
22. ○ A   ○ B   ○ C   ● D   ○ E
23. ○ A   ● B   ○ C   ○ D   ○ E
24. ● A   ○ B   ○ C   ○ D   ○ E
25. ○ A   ○ B   ● C   ○ D   ○ E

Appendix

Preparing Your Students
for Standardized Proficiency Tests

Even as the debate over the value and fairness of standardized tests continues, standardized tests are an annual event for millions of students. In most school districts the results of the tests are vitally important. Scores may be used to determine if students are meeting district or state guidelines, they may be used as a means of comparing the scores of the district's students to local or national norms, or they may be used to decide a student's placement in advanced or remedial classes. No matter how individual scores are used in your school, students deserve the chance to do well. They deserve to be prepared.

By providing students with practice in answering the kinds of questions they will face on a standardized test, an effective program of preparation can familiarize students with testing formats, refresh skills, build confidence, and reduce anxiety, all critical factors that can affect scores as much as basic knowledge. Just like the members of an orchestra rehearse to get ready for a concert, the dancer trains for the big show, and the pianist practices for weeks before the grand recital, preparing students for standardized tests is essential.

To be most effective a test-preparation program should be comprehensive, based on skills your students need to know, and enlist the support of parents. Because students often assume the attitudes of their parents regarding tests—for example, nervous parents frequently make their children anxious—you should seek as much parental involvement in your test preparations as possible. Students who are encouraged by their parents and prepared for tests by their teachers invariably do better than those who come to the testing session with little preparation and support.

WHAT PARENTS NEED TO KNOW
ABOUT STANDARDIZED TESTS

While most parents will agree it is important for their children to do well on standardized tests, many feel there is little they can do to help the outcome. Consequently, aside from encouraging their children to "try your best," they feel there is nothing more for them to do. Much of this feeling arises from parents not fully understanding the testing process.

To provide the parents of your students with information about testing, consider sending home copies of the following reproducibles:

- The Uses of Standardized Tests
- Test Terms
- Common Types of Standardized Tests
- Preparing Your Child for Standardized Tests

You may wish to send these home in a packet with a cover letter (a sample of which is included) announcing the upcoming standardized tests.

THE USES OF STANDARDIZED TESTS

Schools administer standardized tests for a variety of purposes. It is likely that your child's school utilizes the scores of standardized tests in at least some of the following ways.

- Identify strengths and weaknesses in academic skills.

- Identify areas of high interest, ability, or aptitude. Likewise identify areas of average or low ability or aptitude.

- Compare the scores of students within the district to each other as well as to students of other districts. This can be done class to class, school to school, or district to district. Such comparisons help school systems to evaluate their curriculums and plan instruction and programs.

- Provide a basis for comparison of report card grades to national standards.

- Identify students who might benefit from advanced or remedial classes.

- Certify student achievement, for example, in regard to receiving awards.

- Provide reports on student progress.

TEST TERMS

Although standardized tests come in different forms and may be designed to measure different skills, most share many common terms. Understanding these "test terms" is the first step to understanding the tests.

- *Achievement tests* measure how much students have learned in a particular subject area. They concentrate on knowledge of subject matter.

- *Aptitude tests* are designed to predict how well students will do in learning new subject matter in the future. They generally measure a broad range of skills associated with success. Note that the line between aptitude and achievement tests is often indistinct.

- *Battery* refers to a group of tests that are administered during the same testing session. For example, separate tests for vocabulary, language, reading, spelling, and mathematics that comprise an achievement test are known as the *test battery*.

- *Correlation coefficient* is a measure of the strength and direction of the relationship between two items. It can be a positive or negative number.

- *Diagnostic tests* are designed to identify the strengths and weaknesses of students in specific subject areas. They are usually given only to students who show exceptional ability or serious weakness in an area.

- *Grade equivalent scores* are a translation of the score attained on the test to an approximate grade level. Thus, a student whose score translates to a grade level of 4.5 is working at roughly the midyear point of fourth grade. One whose score equals a grade level of 8.0 is able to successfully complete work typically given at the beginning of eighth grade.

- *Individual student profiles* (also referred to as *reports*) display detailed test results for a particular student. Some of these can be so precise that the answer to every question is shown.

- *Item* is a specific question on a test.

- *Mean* is the average of a group of scores.

- *Median* is the middle score in a group of scores.

- *Mode* is the score achieved most by a specific group of test takers.

- *Normal distribution* is a distribution of test scores in which the scores are distributed around the mean and where the mean, median, and mode are the same. A normal distribution, when displayed, appears bell-shaped.

- *Norming population* is the group of students (usually quite large) to whom the test was given and on whose results performance standards for various age or grade levels are based. *Local norms* refer to distributions based on a particular school or school district. *National norms* refer to distributions based on students from around the country.

- *Norm-referenced tests* are tests in which the results of the test may be compared with other norming populations.

- *Percentile rank* is a comparison of a student's raw score with the raw scores of others who took the test. The comparison is most often made with members of the norming population. Percentile rank enables a test taker to see where his or her scores rank among others who take the same test. A percentile rank of 90, for example, means that the test taker scored better than 90% of those who took the test. A percentile rank of 60 means the test taker scored better than 60% of those who took the test. A percentile rank of 30 means he or she scored better than only 30% of those who took the test, and that 70% of the test takers had higher scores.

- *Raw score* is the score of a test based on the number correct. On some tests the raw score may include a correction for guessing.

- *Reliability* is a measure of the degree to which a test measures what it is designed to measure. A test's reliability may be expressed as a reliability coefficient that typically ranges from 0 to 1. Highly reliable tests have reliability coefficients of 0.90 or higher. Reliability coefficients may take several forms. For example, parallel-form reliability correlates the performance on two different forms of a test; split-half reliability correlates two halves of the same test; and test-retest reliability correlates test scores of the same test given at two different times. The producers of standardized tests strive to make them as reliable as possible. Although there are always cases of bright students not doing well on a standardized test and some students who do surprisingly well, most tests are quite reliable and provide accurate results.

- *Score* is the number of correct answers displayed in some form. Sometimes the score is expressed as a *scaled score*, which means that the score provided by the test is derived from the number of correct answers.

- *Standard deviation* is a measure of the variability of test scores. If most scores are near the mean score, the standard deviation will be small; if scores vary widely from the mean, the standard deviation will be large.

- *Standard error of measurement* is an estimate of the amount of possible measurement error in a test. It provides an estimate of how much a student's true test score may vary from the actual score he or she obtained on the test. Tests that have a large standard error of measurement may not accurately reflect a student's true ability. The standard error of measurement is usually small for well-designed tests.

- *Standardized tests* are tests that have been given to students under the same conditions. They are designed to measure the same skills and abilities for everyone who takes them.

- *Stanine scores* are scores expressed between the numbers 1 and 9 with 9 being high.

- *Validity* is the degree to which a test measures what it is supposed to measure. There are different kinds of validity. One, content validity, for example, refers to the degree to which the content of the test is valid for the purpose of the test. Another, predictive validity, refers to the extent to which predictions based on the test are later proven accurate by other evidence.

COMMON TYPES OF STANDARDIZED TESTS

Most standardized tests are broken down into major sections that focus on specific subjects. Together these sections are referred to as a *battery*. The materials and skills tested are based on grade level. The following tests are common throughout the country; however, not all schools administer every test.

- *Analogy tests* measure a student's ability to understand relationships between words (ideas). Here is an example: Boy is to man as girl is to woman. The relationship, of course, is that a boy becomes a man and a girl becomes a woman. Not only does an analogy test the ability to recognize relationships, it tests vocabulary as well.

- *Vocabulary tests* determine whether students understand the meaning of certain words. They are most often based on the student's projected grade-level reading, comprehension, and spelling skills.

- *Reading comprehension tests* show how well students can understand reading passages. These tests appear in many different formats. In most, students are required to read a passage and then answer questions designed to measure reading ability.

- *Spelling tests* show spelling competence, based on grade-level appropriate words. The tests may require students to select a correctly spelled word from among misspelled words, or may require students to find the misspelled word among correctly spelled words.

- *Language mechanics tests* concentrate on capitalization and punctuation. Students may be required to find examples of incorrect capitalization and punctuation as well as examples of correct capitalization and punctuation in sentences and short paragraphs.

- *Language expression tests* focus on the ability of students to use words correctly according to the standards of conventional English. In many "expression" tests, effective structuring of ideas is also tested.

- *Writing tests* determine how effectively students write and can express their ideas. Usually a topic is given and students must express their ideas on the topic.

Common Types of Standardized Tests *(Continued)*

- *Mathematics problem-solving tests* are based on concepts and applications, and assess the ability of students to solve math problems. These tests often include sections on number theory, interpretation of data and graphs, and logical analysis.

- *Mathematics computation tests* measure how well students can add, subtract, multiply, and divide. While the difficulty of the material depends on grade level, these tests generally cover whole numbers, fractions, decimals, percents, and geometry.

- *Science tests* measure students' understanding of basic science facts.

- *Social studies tests* measure students' understanding of basic facts in social studies.

PREPARING YOUR CHILD
FOR STANDARDIZED TESTS

As a parent, there is much you can do to help your son or daughter get ready for taking a standardized test.

During the weeks leading up to the test . . .

- Attend parent-teacher conferences and find out how you can help your child succeed in school.

- Assume an active role in school. Seeing your commitment to his or her school enhances the image of school in your child's eyes.

- Find out when standardized tests are given and plan accordingly. For example, avoid scheduling doctor or dentist appointments for your child during the testing dates. Students who take standardized tests with their class usually do better than students who make up tests because of absences.

- Monitor your child's progress in school. Make sure your child completes his or her homework and projects. Support good study habits and encourage your child to always do his or her best.

- Encourage your child's creativity and interests. Provide plenty of books, magazines, and educational opportunities.

- Whenever you speak of standardized tests, speak of them in a positive manner. Emphasize that while these tests are important, it is not the final score that counts, but that your child tries his or her best.

During the days immediately preceding the test . . .

- Once the test has been announced, discuss the test with your child to relieve apprehension. Encourage your son or daughter to take the test seriously, but avoid being overly anxious. (Sometimes parents are more nervous about their children's tests than the kids are.)

- Help your child with any materials his or her teacher sends home in preparation for the test.

- Make sure your child gets a good night's sleep each night before a testing day.

- On the morning of the test, make sure your child wakes up on time, eats a solid breakfast, and arrives at school on time.

- Remind your child to listen to the directions of the teacher carefully and to read directions carefully.

- Encourage your child to do his or her best.

COVER LETTER TO PARENTS
ANNOUNCING STANDARDIZED TESTS

Use the following letter to inform the parents of your students about upcoming standardized tests in your school. Feel free to adjust the letter according to your needs.

Dear Parents/Guardians,

On _____ (dates) _____ , our

class will be taking the _____ (name of test) _____ .

During the next few weeks students will work on various practice tests to help

prepare for the actual test.

You can help, too. Please read the attached materials and discuss the

importance of the tests with your child. By supporting your child's efforts in

preparation, you can help him or her attain the best possible scores.

Thank you.

Sincerely,

(Name)

WHAT STUDENTS NEED TO KNOW
ABOUT STANDARDIZED TESTS

The mere thought of taking a standardized test frightens many students, causing a wide range of symptoms from mild apprehension to upset stomachs and panic attacks. Since even low levels of anxiety can distract students and undermine their achievement, you should attempt to lessen their concerns.

Apprehension, anxiety, and fear are common responses to situations that we perceive as being out of our control. When students are faced with a test on which they don't know what to expect, they may worry excessively that they won't do well. Such emotions, especially when intense, almost guarantee that they will make careless mistakes. When students are prepared properly for a test, they are more likely to know "what to expect." This reduces negative emotions and students are able to enter the testing situation with confidence, which almost always results in better scores.

The first step to preparing your students for standardized tests is to mention the upcoming tests well in advance—at least a few weeks ahead of time—and explain that in the days leading up to the test, the class will be preparing. Explain that while they will not be working with the actual test, the work they will be doing is designed to help them get ready. You may wish to use the analogy of a sports team practicing during the pre-season. Practices help players sharpen their skills, anticipate game situations, and build confidence. Practicing during the pre-season helps athletes perform better during the regular season.

You might find it useful to distribute copies of the following reproducibles:

- Test-taking Tips for Students
- Test Words You Should Know

Hand these out a few days before the testing session. Go over them with your students and suggest that they take them home and ask their parents to review the sheets with them on the night before the test.

TEST-TAKING TIPS FOR STUDENTS

1. Try your best.

2. Be confident and think positively. People who believe they will do well usually do better than those who are not confident.

3. Fill out the answer sheet correctly. Be careful that you darken all "circles." Be sure to use a number 2 pencil unless your teacher tells you otherwise.

4. Listen carefully to all directions and follow them exactly. If you don't understand something, ask your teacher.

5. Read all questions and their possible answers carefully. Sometimes an answer may at first seem right, but it isn't. Always read all answers before picking one.

6. Try to answer the questions in order, but don't waste too much time on hard questions. Go on to easier ones and then go back to the hard ones.

7. Don't be discouraged by hard questions. On most tests for every hard question there are many easy ones.

8. Try not to make careless mistakes.

9. Budget your time and work quickly.

10. Be sure to fill in the correct answer spaces on your answer sheet. Use a finger of your non-writing hand to keep your place on the answer space.

11. Look for clues and key words when answering questions.

12. If you become "stuck" on a question, eliminate any answers you know are wrong and then make your best guess of the remaining answers. (Do this only if there is no penalty for guessing. Check with your teacher about this.)

13. Don't leave any blanks. Guess if you are running out of time. (Only do this if unanswered questions are counted wrong. Check with your teacher.)

14. Double-check your work if time permits.

15. Erase completely any unnecessary marks on your answer sheet.

TEST WORDS YOU SHOULD KNOW

The words below are used in standardized tests. Understanding what each one means will help you when you take your test.

all	double-check	opposite
always	end	order
answer sheet	error	oval
best	example	part
blank	fill in	passage
booklet	finish	pick
bubble	following	punctuation
capitalization	go on	question
check	item	read
choose	language expression	reread
circle	language mechanics	right
column	mark	row
complete	match	same as
comprehension	missing	sample
continue	mistake	section
correct	name	select
definition	never	stop
details	none	topic
directions	not true	true
does not belong	number 2 pencil	vocabulary

CREATING A POSITIVE
TEST-TAKING ENVIRONMENT

Little things really do matter when students take standardized tests. Students who are consistently encouraged to do their best throughout the year in the regular classroom generally achieve higher scores on standardized tests than students who maintain a careless attitude regarding their studies. Of course, motivating students to do their best is an easy thing to suggest, but not such an easy goal to accomplish.

There are, fortunately, some steps you can take to foster positive attitudes on the part of your students in regard to standardized tests. Start by discussing the test students will take, and explain how the results of standardized tests are used. When students understand the purpose of testing, they are more likely to take the tests seriously. Never speak of tests in a negative manner, for example, saying that students must work hard or they will do poorly. Instead, speak in positive terms: by working hard and trying their best they will achieve the best results.

To reduce students' concerns, assure them that the use of practice tests will improve their scores. Set up a thorough test-preparation schedule well in advance of the tests, based upon the needs and abilities of your students. Avoid cramming preparation into the last few days before the test. Cramming only burdens students with an increased workload and leads to anxiety and worry. A regular, methodical approach to preparation is best, because this enables you to check for weaknesses in skills and offer remediation.

The value of preparation for standardized tests cannot be understated. When your students feel that they are prepared for the tests, and that you have confidence in them, they will feel more confident and approach the tests with a positive frame of mind. Along with effective instruction throughout the year, a focused program of test preparation will help ensure that your students will have the chance to achieve their best scores on standardized tests.